Chronic degenerative diseases flood the American healthcare system with sufferers. In spite of modern medicine's ability to reduce symptoms of many illnesses, their fundamental causes—and cures— still elude traditional practitioners. Because toxic heavy metals are associated with our two biggest challenges, cancer and heart disease (as well as many other severe disease states), the etiology of heavy metal toxicity must be recognized *and* addressed. Chelation is the answer. A therapy whose time has come, chelation should now be defined and understood as a 21st century modality of choice for removing toxic metals from the body.

Some of the world's best known therapies and treatments were not accepted in their early days. For example, acceptance of vitamin C's benefits as a powerful antioxidant took a long time to influence traditional viewpoints. While chelation therapy with EDTA is in its infancy, it will prove as a powerful agent for the removal of toxic heavy metals. I also encourage all clinicians to get on board with this amazing modality.

Intravenous chelation has been recognized for decades by the United States Food and Drug Administration as the treatment of choice for lead poisoning. Since intravenous chelation is time consuming and expensive, I've been administering chelation in the form of a suppository, and believe it is a revolutionary advancement. I've seen excellent results for over ten years with thousands of my patients and within the last three years I decided to study calcium disodium EDTA suppositories. I have now published proven results of its safety and efficacy in approved clinical trials.

Working with a combined approach that repairs cell membrane damage caused by oxidative stress and revitalizing cell membranes with targeted nutrition, suppository chelation works to improve and sometimes halt disease conditions.

Expand your view and learn about this breakthrough technology. It will forever change your perspective on today's paradigm of practicing medicine.

--Rita R. Ellithorpe, MD

Table of Contents

Page

Preface.. 1

Chapter I
Heavy Metal Toxicity: A Root of Many Ills................. 4

Chapter II
Chelation Therapy: That was Then; This is Now........... 23

Chapter III
Testing for Heavy Metals: Eliminate the Bad and Ugly... 36

Chapter IV
The Toxic Metal Connection to Major Diseases............ 53

Chapter V
Discovering a Better Way to Chelate........................ 66

Chapter VI
Cutting Edge Combo Therapy................................ 80

Chapter VII
Actual Case Studies... 91

Chapter VIII
The Bright Future of Chelation Therapy.................... 98

Additional Resources.. 110

Chapter I
Heavy Metal Toxicity: A Root of Many Ills

Even though I have been practicing medicine for nearly 30 years, I am continually amazed at the body's ability to heal itself. As a physician, my goal is to give the body the tools it needs to gently guide the intrinsic wisdom of its basic and foundational unit of life, the cell. Each cell is unique and plays a specific role. Cells communicate through cell surface membrane biochemical pathways that support health of the total being. A divinely created order has arranged cells into tissues, tissues into organs, and those organs into systems to make up your body. If your cells and their surface membranes are healthy, then you will experience optimal energy and vitality!

The anatomy of a cell
Each cell is like a mini-person. The membrane surrounding each healthy cell is designed to pull in nutrition, keep out undesirable toxins and pathogens (such as bacteria and viruses), and provide an outlet for waste elimination. Internally, the cell has a "brain" called the nucleus that directs and regulates its daily activities. There are several "fuel centers" in each cell called mitochondria that are responsible for giving the cell the energy it needs to carry out its unique and special roles. Various other organelles (sub-units) within the cell assist it in its tasks.

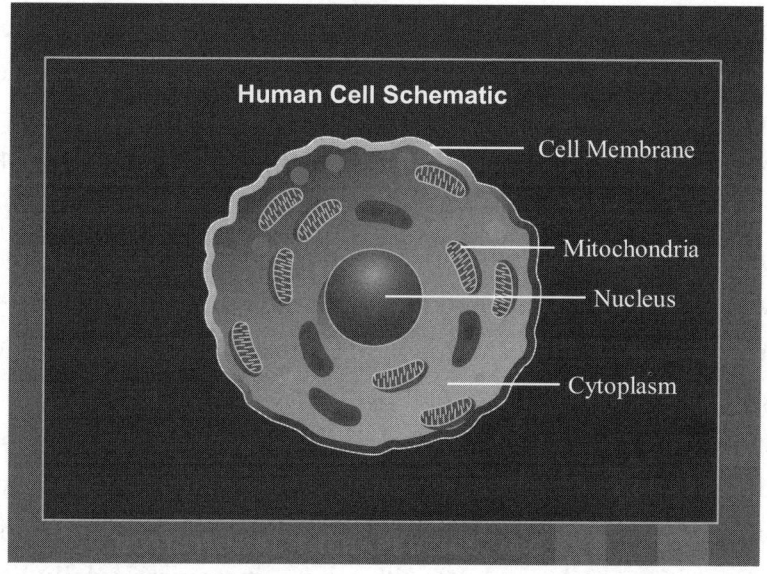

The daily routine of life runs smoothly for the cell (and the entire body) when the transport of nutrition into—and excretion of wastes from—the cell takes place normally, efficiently and without interruption. However, there are constant negative forces at work on the cell to destroy its routine.

Like a metaphor for life, there are harmful agents that daily try to break down the cell's defenses to annihilate and overcome it. The most pervasive of these are substances called free radicals.

Free radicals: pirates of the cell membrane
Free radicals are byproducts of metabolism (the energy expended to support the body's daily activities) like maintaining a temperature of 98.6°, cellular repair, or even the vitality needed to read this page! These molecules are unstable because they are missing an electron. Where complete oxygen atoms contain a

nucleus with paired electrons orbiting around it, a free radical has only one electron. These incomplete renegade molecules then seek to make themselves "whole" by robbing cell membranes of their electrons. By stealing the electron from another molecule, the free radical creates another free radical. This imbalanced situation leads to an ever-perpetuating chain reaction of cellular damage—which has been compared to an internal atomic explosion—accelerating the disease and aging process. But the good news is, you can minimize the rate of damage with good nutrition. However, it's not a one-shot deal. It's like doing dishes. You can't do them once and expect to never do them again. They must be washed on a consistent basis. And so it is with a regular program of nutrition intake and detoxification—it requires a daily lifestyle to support cellular repair.

Where the real action starts
The cell membrane is made up of specialized lipids (fats). The molecules of this membrane are, unfortunately, very susceptible to "oxidative damage" from free radicals. This is where the cell membrane is literally being burned. Free radicals trigger a chemical reaction called lipid peroxidation, which causes the cell membrane to stiffen. This condition harms the ability of the cell membrane to accept nutrients, receive signals from other cells, or eliminate waste products. Many other cellular activities and molecules can be affected, as well—including RNA, DNA and protein enzymes.

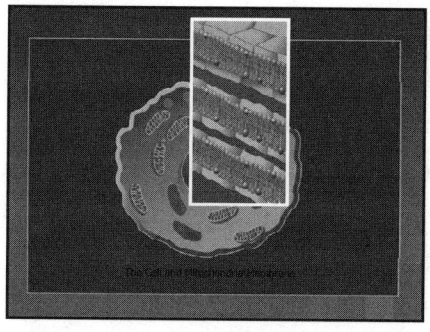 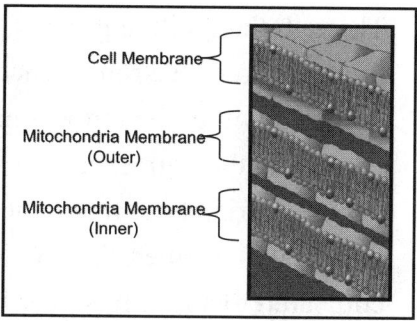

Today we have to cope with an ever-increasing load of toxins in this industrial 21st century. They include air pollutants and heavy metal contaminants. However, nearly 100 years of evidence shows that a process known as chelation can effectively address our modern heavy metal issues. Free radicals produced in the cell itself comprise only a fraction of the "oxidative stress" load with which the cell must cope. Other sources of free radicals include air pollutants and exposure to heavy metal contaminants. These renegade molecules oxidize or burn holes in the cell membranes and this action can lead to cell death.

If only we would be as concerned about free radicals and their impact on the membranes of our cells as we are about putting on sunscreen to protect our skin! The action is similar and it's just as important to our health.

Once free radicals breach the cell's membrane barrier—its first line of defense— they target the secondary lipid-rich membranes surrounding the mitochondria, the cell's power plant. The mitochondria take in fats and carbohydrates and with the oxygen we breathe, transforms these substances into vital energy.

Through the ignition process, some of the combusted oxygen produces free electrons, generating free radicals. They are then funneled within the mitochondria in a kind of feedback loop, producing the high energy bond of ATP. Within the confine of the mitochondria, these free radicals are useful. However, outside of this safety chamber, they wreak havoc. This scenario can be compared to a fire. It is very beneficial inside the regulated space of a fireplace, keeping a home warm. But if it starts a fire on the sofa, it will consume the home. Likewise, if free radicals breach the delicate membranes of the mitochondria, they can also attack the nucleus, the command center of the cell and its cellular blueprint, the DNA. The DNA is the instruction book which tells the cell, biochemically, how to function. The cell has the ability to fix much of the damage done to nuclear DNA; however, wounded mitochondrial DNA is not as easy to repair.

Injury to mitochondrial DNA accumulates over time. It interferes with the cell's energy and is very serious. This can be compared to giving you a heart attack. The cell then dies and the body is on a fast track to disease and premature aging. Free radical damage, therefore, is a basic route of tissue injury—by first wounding or killing the cell. The damage arising from a cell can then spread to nearby cells, tissues, organs and systems that may finally overwhelm the body, causing a chronic disease state leading to death.

We are all slowly burning to death (or more quickly if you ignore the information in this book!). So now, let's stop or slow down the burn from heavy metal fires. Chelation is like calling the fire department to remove the burning embers, the burning embers constantly touching your cell membranes. This is literally the roof of your cellular home. Heavy metals in your body compound free radical generation many fold—thousands and possibly even several million—times over. When free radicals bump into toxic metal atoms, they literally explode in both activity and quantity. Like a small ember sets an entire house on fire, a small blaze of free radicals generates a huge blaze of cell membrane oxidation. Therefore, it makes sense that when you remove toxic metals (these burning embers) from the body, you greatly minimize the number and damage of free radicals they can recruit. I will explain the ways you can guard against free radicals later in this book.

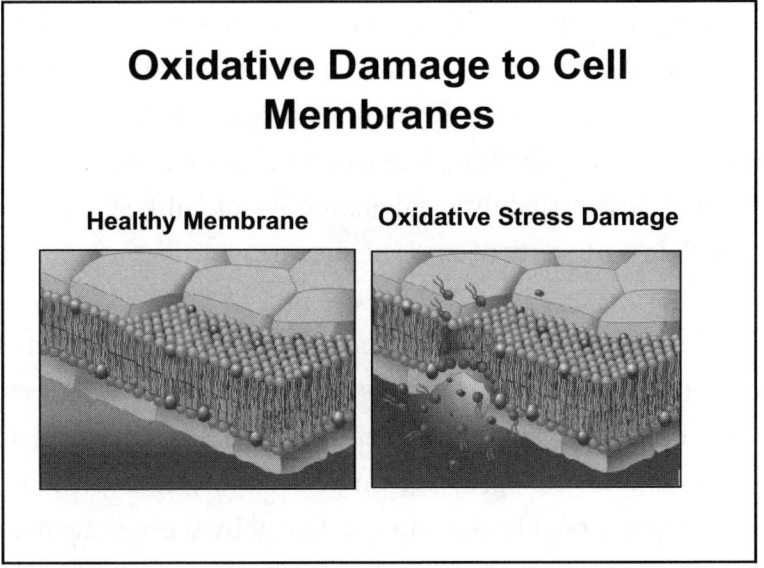

Oxidative Damage to Cell Membranes

Healthy Membrane   **Oxidative Stress Damage**

Always in your face

Exposure to heavy metals comes from different sources: the environment, in dust of the air you breathe, medications, personal care products, your water, and even your food. The three principal routes of entry are: the mouth, lungs, and skin. There are many heavy metals that decimate cell membrane health, but the major ones are mercury, lead, aluminum, cadmium and arsenic.

Heavy metal toxicity is not a new phenomenon. History is replete with cases of heavy metal poisonings and even books and movies have been written about them. The term "mad as a hatter" was first coined in Lewis Carroll's classic book "Alice in Wonderland." This saying originated because of the hat-making industry. During the 1800s, a mercury solution was commonly employed to help turn fur into felt. The hatters breathed the toxic mercury fumes and the accumulation of this deadly metal in their bodies caused trembling, loss of coordination, slurred speech, memory loss, irritability and anxiety—not unlike the presenting complaints of many of my patients.

The fall and demise of the Roman Empire has been blamed partly on lead poisoning from goblets and lead pipes used in homes of the aristocrats. Could these neurotoxic effects have been a factor in the senate's collapse? We might seriously consider that some of our congressional leadership is affected by these same maladies. Our leadership of today has to consider the impact of lead, as well as other synergistic heavy metal sources.

It is reported that Beethoven's hair was tested and found to contain very high concentrations of lead. It is suggested that this could account for his deafness, colic-like abdominal pain, irritability and depression.

Heavy metal hang-outs

Heavy metals are found in sources of all shapes, sizes and varieties. The following is an abbreviated scope of where these harmful toxins are found.

- Adhesives
- Air conditioner filters
- Aluminum foil
- Aluminum cookware
- Amalgam dental fillings
- Antacids (aluminum)
- Antibiotics (various metals)
- Antiperspirants, deodorants
- Auto brake linings (lead, cadmium, antimony)
- Auto exhaust
- Baking powder
- Batteries
- Beer (arsenic)
- Bleached flour
- Body lotions and creams (many)
- Calomel (talcum powder)
- Cake Mixes (aluminum)
- Canned goods (lead)
- Ceramic plates, cookware
- Chlorine bleaches (mercury)
- Cigarettes
- Coal burning power plants (mercury)
- Cooking utensils
- Coffee (cadmium)
- Coffee creamers (non-dairy)
- Corn bread (aluminum)
- Cosmetics (most)
- Cotton buds (mercury)

- Dental bridges (aluminum)
- Diuretics (mercury)
- Dolomite (arsenic)
- Douches (aluminum)
- Eye liner (antimony)
- Fabric softeners (mercury)
- Fish
- Fertilizers
- Flour tortillas (aluminum)
- Fluoridated water
- Food additives (aluminum)
- Fungicides, herbicides, pesticides
- Hair color restorer and rinses (lead)
- Hemorrhoid suppositories (mercury)
- Household lawn, garden chemicals
- Hydrogenated oils (nickel, cadmium)
- Icing sugar (aluminum)
- Inks used by printers and tattooist (mercury)
- Instant soup powders
- Laundry aids (arsenic)
- Laxatives (mercury)
- Medications, anti-inflammatory and pain (aluminum)
- Mercurial diuretics (mercury)
- Metal watch bands (nickel)
- Microwave popcorn (aluminum)
- Milk and cream powders
- Paint pigments and solvents
- Pizza crust(aluminum)
- Prescription drugs (some)
- Processed cheese
- Refined grains (cadmium)
- Rice (cadmium)
- Rubber toys (lead)
- Salt (mercury)
- Sanitary towels (mercury)
- Selsun Blue shampoo (selenium-toxic in high doses)

- Skin lotions (aluminum)
- Soaps
- Soft drinks (cadmium)
- Solvents
- Some paints
- Stain resistant material (arsenic)
- Storage batteries (lead)
- Sewage sludge (mercury-used widely for agriculture)
- Suntan lotions
- Table salt (aluminum)
- Tap water
- Tin cans
- Tobacco smoke (arsenic)
- Toothpicks (mercury)
- Topical disinfectants (mercurochrome, merthiolate) (mercury)
- Various occupations
- Water running through lead pipes (lead)
- Water softeners (cadmium)
- Wood preservatives (mercury)

Note: Aluminumized baking powder is now being used in many foods that were formerly prepared without baking powder, such as pizza crust, raised doughnuts, pie crusts, cookies, waffles, prepared meats, cheeses, and other products that were once aluminum-free.

Case in point: lead poisoning

Lead is a very prevalent heavy metal and is very damaging to the cells. Even low levels of lead have been clearly linked to the increased incidence of cancer and heart disease. Paint manufacturers once used lead as a white pigment and drying agent, and the dust from it is a primary contaminant in people living in older homes. Lead impairs functioning of many organs, especially the kidneys, the liver, the heart, and the brain. Exposure of pregnant women and children between the ages of 1 and 6 can especially trigger devastating long-term mental health effects. Lead interferes with functioning of the brain's prefrontal lobe, the area that controls impulsivity, long-range thinking and communication skills. Scientists feel that even low blood-lead levels (such as 5 micrograms per deciliter) can harm a child, including decreasing potential IQ. This condition can set the stage for future criminal behavior, since it stimulates impulsivity and aggression.

So lead poisoning not only causes extreme health problems, it has also been implicated as one aspect of today's social ills, as well. Consider the following information. An online newspaper article published out of Baltimore describes a young man of 22 who was serving a 35-year term for the gruesome murder of his uncle and had recently been charged with strangling a 16-year-old fellow inmate. A previous report listing several health conditions suffered by the young convict, Kevin G. Johns Jr., included lead poisoning.

The story also highlights the work of Dr. Herbert Needleman, a pediatrician and child psychiatrist at the University of Pittsburgh Medical Center, who was one of the first scientists to study the connection between lead poisoning and anti-social behavior. Dr. Needleman was concerned because mothers of children with high lead levels often complained about their children's behavioral problems, including that of being aggressive and difficult to control.

Needleman's initial research, conducted in 1979, found 'significant difference in the lead levels with children who had attention or behavioral problems.' Next, he investigated the correlation between lead and anti-social behavior. In testing the bone-lead levels of 194 children in the Allegheny County, Pa., juvenile justice system in 1998, he compared the convicted youths to a control group of 146 students living in the same county with no criminal record. He called his results 'startling' because the convicted youths had lead levels 10 to 11 times higher than the control group. Needleman added that 'there is no doubt that lead affects important functions of controlling impulses, and I believe this relates to crime.' Other research supports Dr. Needleman's discovery that lead is linked to anti-social behavior. The article goes on to report that:

"In 2001, scientists Paul Stretesky and Michael Lynch used federal data that measured lead levels in the air in 3,111 counties across the United States. Comparing the data to the homicide rates for the same counties, the scientists found that the counties with the highest rate of lead-air pollution had four times as many homicides than the counties with the lowest.

"Rick Nevin, an economic consultant, was hired by the federal Department of Housing and Urban Development to find out the cost of removing lead paint from public housing. Concurrently, he studied the link between lead exposure and violent crime and his research revealed that lead-exposure rates of American children between 1941 and 1986 matched with national fluctuations in violent crime rates, including robbery and aggravated assault. Nevins found that blood-lead levels in children were predictors for the violent crime rate two decades later, when those children would be adults.

"Deborah Denno, a law professor at Fordham University School of Law, analyzed data from a long-term government study that followed 487 boys in Philadelphia from age 0 to age 22. She sifted through more than 3,000 variables to find facts that correlated to incarceration and criminality. Denno found that elevated blood-lead levels to be 'the strongest predictor of disciplinary problems in school kids and the third-strongest predictor of juvenile crime. One of the other two strongest predictors of juvenile crime, previous disciplinary problems, relates back to lead, too.'"

We used to think that lead exposure in children came primarily from old buildings shedding peeling paint and from breathing the dust residue. Now we have another concern: fluoridated water. In 1999, a press release from Dartmouth University in New Hampshire titled "Study Finds Correlation between Fluorides in Water and Lead Levels," reported that, in a survey analysis of over 280,000 Massachusetts children, the investigators found that silicofluorides—chemicals widely used in treating public water supplies—are associated with an increase in children's absorption of lead. When compared to a similar group of 30 towns that did not use silicofluorides, children in 30 communities that use these chemicals were more than twice as likely to have over 10 micrograms of lead per deciliter of blood.

Roger Masters, awarded the position of Nelson A. Rockefeller Professor of Government Emeritus at Dartmouth College, headed the study. He emphasized that "Silicofluorides are largely untested," emphasizing that over 90 percent of America's fluoridated drinking water supplies are treated with silicofluorides. "Virtually all research on fluoridation safety has focused on sodium fluoride, even though the studies in the 1930s showed important biological differences between these two chemicals. The [silicofluorides] correlation with [lead] blood levels is especially serious because lead poisoning is associated with higher rates of learning disabilities, hyperactivity, substance abuse and crime."

Symptoms of heavy metal toxicity:

- Decreased intelligence in children
- Nervous system disorders
- Immune dysfunctions
- Depression
- Fatigue
- Muscle weakness and aches
- Anemia
- Skin rashes
- High blood pressure
- Diarrhea
- Nausea
- Metallic taste in mouth
- Irritability
- Tremors
- Cancer
- Hyperactivity
- Autism
- Behavioral disorders
- Headaches
- Aggression
- Violence

Although some elimination is achieved in the feces, urine and sweat, these pathways are minimal and ineffectual for the cell's protection.

Cancer links

The body can't use heavy metals for any beneficial purpose, so it warehouses them in the most inert or inactive tissue (i.e. fat, ligaments and especially bones) and they silently accumulate over time.

Of course, the acute exposure of significant amounts in chips of lead paint can be measured in the blood shortly after exposure and found to be elevated. But we were never taught in medical school (or considered) the damage caused by smaller, daily accumulations. Back in the 1970s, the World Health Organization (WHO) established 60 micrograms of lead per deciliter as a toxic level. However, with more scientific knowledge, that amount has been reduced to 30 micrograms per deciliter.

And here is the greatest misunderstanding: The body tucks away the accumulations, and even though serum levels don't reflect more than 30mcg/dcl, there is far more damage going on in these sites. Again, the body is normally equipped to automatically flush out various toxins at their onset, but today's world is so polluted, the body's detoxification pathways are often overwhelmed. Therefore—as a defense mechanism—it resorts to storing heavy metals for possible elimination at some future time. When it can't, however, degenerative diseases ensue. The body's inherent detoxification pathways were not designed to handle heavy metals at our current levels of daily exposure, nor can our immune system destroy them.

In every random blood sample for heavy metal toxicities (and I have sampled thousands), I have observed that all patients (to date) carry a measurable body burden of various types of heavy metals. Remember, this sampling measures the metals flowing in the blood that are in equilibrium with the toxic metals sequestered in tissue sites such as bone, fat, ligaments, etc. Sequestered heavy metals are no longer considered safe or non-problematic. We each have sixty-three trillion cells in our bodies containing twenty-three pairs of genetic (DNA) strands. Free radicals constantly bombard this genetic blueprint material and this action can change the DNA of cells and mitochondria. If the body is unable to repair the resulting mutations, a disease state may occur or the cell can die.

It has been shown that mutations must take place on both strands of DNA around the same time for cancer to occur. The body usually repairs at least one strand, minimizing the chances for cancer. However, heavy metal toxicity—such as that from lead alone—greatly increases the probability of cancer because it generates so many free radicals at the same time. Antioxidants are nutrients that contribute electrons to free radicals, halting their devastating rampage. However, their sphere of influence is limited. The free radical-generating heavy metals must be eliminated for long-term positive health effects.

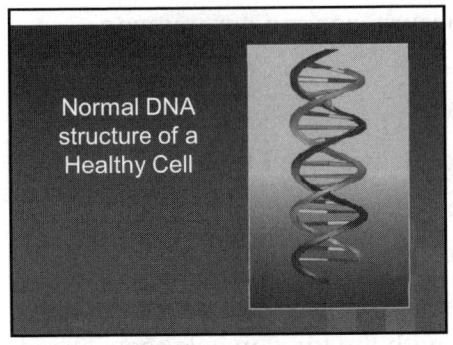

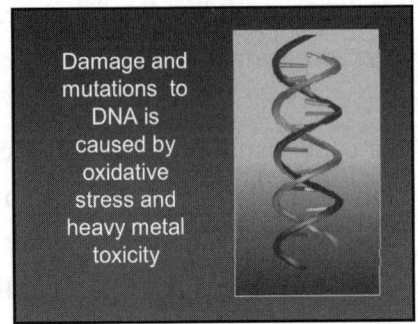

Low levels of heavy metals cause cumulative damage to the gastrointestinal, immune, nervous, cardiovascular and reproductive systems. Consider these topics in the news:

- 45 states have issued mercury advisories over coal-fired power plants
- Mercury and fish advisories issued for waterways
- Dangerous lead levels found in homes
- Lead linked to premature deaths in adults
- CDC vaccine data leads scientists to shocking discovery of autism link
- FDA warns pregnant women to limit ingestion of tuna

And the random blood samples from my patients consistently showed contamination from at least three or more metals besides lead, the most common being cadmium, arsenic and mercury. According to published articles in medical journals, chronic low levels of lead are being linked to our two biggest killers: cancer and heart disease. One study shows that "in a nationally representative sample of the U.S. population, blood lead levels as low as 5–9 micrograms per deciliter were associated with an increased risk of death from all causes, cardiovascular disease, and cancer."

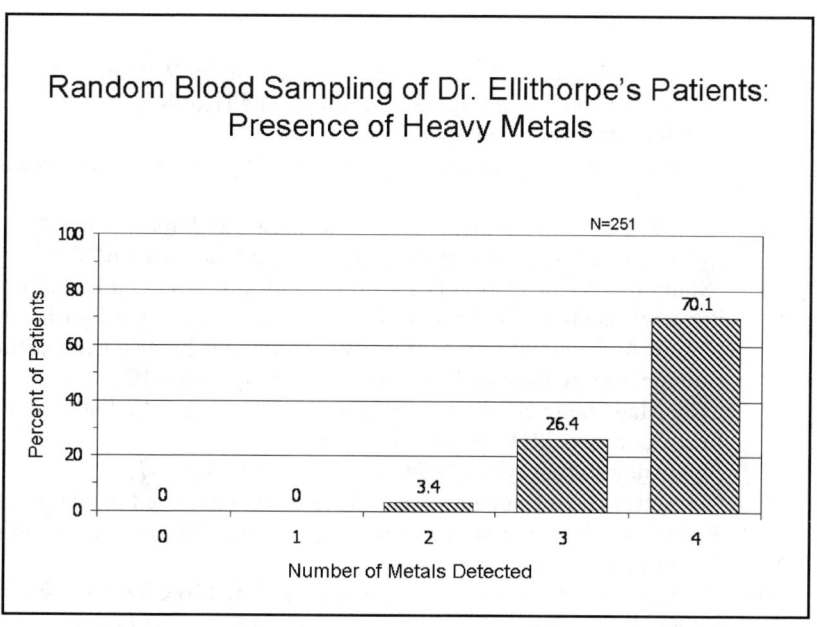

Random Blood Sampling of Dr. Ellithorpe's Patients: Presence of Heavy Metals

What you can do

The answer to halting and reversing this pervasive problem lies in removing the heavy metals, then repairing the damaged cell membrane and revitalizing the body. I use some excellent products in my practice that have given my patients amazing results and a new lease on life. I first give my patients a special product that removes the heavy metals, then I employ nutrition to replenish the damaged cell lipid membranes and keep the cells healthy and strong. My patients who undergo this multi-dimensional modality report more energy, less depression, their aches and pains diminish or resolve and their lab reports reflect less cell damage markers, such as sedimentation (SED) rates, HS-CRP and others. Read about the remarkable key component of this breakthrough combination therapy later in this book!

References

1. Press Conference October 17, 2000. Statement by William J. Walsh, Ph.D. Director of Beethoven Research Project. The Health Research Institute and Pfeiffer Treatment Center, Naperville, Illinois.(www.sjsu.edu/depts/beethoven/hair/hairtestpc.html; accessed 6/17/07).
2. "Full of Lead" by Stephen Janis. Baltimore City Paper; 3/9/2005. (www.citypaper.com/printStory.asp?id=9738; accessed 6/26/07).
3. "Study Finds Correlation Between Fluorides in Water and Lead Levels." Press release from Dartmouth News; August 31, 1999. Roger Masters, Nelson A. Rockefeller Professor of Government Emeritus at Dartmouth College. (www.fluoridation.com/lead.htm; accessed 4/23/07).
4. "The Mad Hatter Syndrome: mercury and biological toxicity" by Leigh Erin Connealy, MD. January 06, 2006. (www.newstarget.com/016544.html; accessed 4/23/07).
5. "45 States Have Issued Mercury Advisories: coal-fired power plants." Source: Environmental Protection Agency and Department of Natural Resources.
6. "Mercury and Fish Advisories Issued for Nine More Waterways. Source: De Ridder Beauregard Daily News. Quoted from The Louisiana Department of Health and Hospitals Environmental Quality.
7. "Dangerous Lead Levels Found in More Homes." Source: Cincinnati Enquirer. Quoted from the EPA.
8. "Lead Linked to Premature Deaths in Adults: Early Exposure = 46% Higher Mortality." Source: The Baltimore Sun. Quoted from the CDC.
9. "California Sues Over Heavy Metal Fish." Source: Business Report. Quoted from the California Attorney General.
10. "EPA Doubles Estimates of Children with Mercury in Blood." Source: The News-Press. Quoted from Department of Environmental Protection.
11. "CDC Vaccine Data Leads Scientists to Shocking Discovery: Possible Autism/Neurological Link." Source: Yahoo News—Quoted from the CDC.
12. "Chromated Copper Arsenate: CCA-Treated Lumber Poses Danger from Arsenic." *Toxico Sci.* 2004 Jun;79(2):287-95.
13. "FDA Warns Pregnant Women to Limit Tuna." Source: Richard Simmons; Los Angeles Times.3/2004.
14. Schober SE, Mirel LB, Graubard BI, Brody DJ, Flegal KM. Blood Lead Levels and Death from All Causes, Cardiovascular Disease, and Cancer: Results from the NHANES III Mortality Study. *Environ Health Perspect.* 2006 October, 114(10): 1538-1541.

Chapter II
Chelation Therapy: That was Then; This is Now

We are swimming daily in a sea of heavy metal toxins. Even before babies leave the womb, they are tainted with multiple pollutants via their mothers' exposures and accumulations. From mercury-contaminated fish to mercury in vaccines, dental fillings, and calamine lotion, to cadmium spewing from car exhaust and cigarette smoke, we are awash in a flood of heavy metal pollution. Cadmium is even an energy source for your cell phone and laptop! This heavy metal toxin has also been linked to kidney and prostate cancer, among many other cancers.

Heavy metals also fall out of the sky. Did you know that nearly 5,000 jet aircraft pass over the United States on any given day and the jet fuel exhaust is replete with several heavy metals? You can't avoid it; you can't get away from it; but you can *cleanse your body* from these insidious poisons through a detoxification method called chelation therapy.

Chelation therapy is a method of removing heavy metals from the body by binding them with chelating agents. Currently, the most widely recognized chelating compound is an artificial amino acid known as ethylene diamine tetraacetic acid (EDTA). "Chele" (pronounced kelay) is the Greek word for claw and the chemical chelating molecule is "C" or claw shaped. It seizes a positively charged metal ion and surrounds it. This action inactivates the metal, then the body safely eliminates the bound compound, primarily via the kidneys. To visualize this concept, imagine pinching a marble between the thumb and forefinger, the marble being the metal ion and the thumb and forefinger being the chelating agent.

Because EDTA has an affinity to heavy particles, it can attract and bind to heavy metals. The toxic ion and the amino acid connect and then—because the body regards the EDTA as a foreign substance—it sends it to the kidney for elimination. Both the EDTA and the heavy metals get a free ride into the toilet.

Chelation is used in many commercial, as well as medical, applications. You see chelating principles in action every time you wash clothes. The chelating ingredients in household detergents prevent soap scum from leaving a residue on your laundry or the washing machine.

Following is a history timeline describing the way the principle of chelation began and how it has evolved into the medical arena to help reclaim health and rescue lives.

Early history of chelation therapy
Although EDTA was used many years before, it wasn't until the 1940s that it was introduced into the medical arena.

World War II—Professor R.A. Peters and his associates at Oxford University used a chelating compound called BAL

(British Anti-Lewisite) to make arsenic from poison gases less harmful.

1947—Martin Rubin, Ph.D., of Georgetown University collaborated with a graduate student named Peter Weiss. It turned out to be a strategic alliance and the Berswerth Chemical Company provided research grant money to Georgetown University so that they could study EDTA's ability to chelate calcium.

The first medicinal use of EDTA was introduced by Charles Geschickter, M.D., a clinical colleague of Rubin, at Georgetown University in Washington. They administered nickel-EDTA to a breast cancer patient without causing beneficial or harmful effects. They subsequently observed that the nickel-EDTA compound was eliminated via the urine, unchanged: not conclusively beneficial, but not harmful, either.

1950s—In the early 1950s, interest and research in the medicinal use of chelation soared. A group of Michigan factory workers poisoned by lead batteries and U.S. sailors painting ships and other facilities with lead paint were successfully chelated with EDTA. By the mid-1950s chelation was recognized as the premier treatment for lead poisoning in both children and adults.

Around this same time, the benefits of EDTA chelation therapy in treating heart disease was introduced by Norman E. Clarke Sr., M.D., F.A.C.C., a renowned cardiologist and chief of research at the Providence Hospital in Detroit, Michigan. He theorized that because EDTA binds calcium, it might eliminate calcium deposits from inside blood vessels. Even though Dr. Clarke and his colleagues were the first to test his hypothesis through clinical studies on patients with heart disease, he later realized that chelation's primary benefit was in binding heavy metals that damage body tissues.

Dr. Albert J. Boyle, professor of chemistry, and Dr. Gordon B. Myers, professor of medicine, both of Wayne State University in Detroit, helped Dr. Clarke conduct early research on patients with coronary disease. They worked with the worst cases and brought them back to health. After chelation therapy, individuals suffering from advanced atherosclerotic cardiovascular ailments enjoyed improved skin color, normal circulation in their extremities, improved muscular coordination and brain function, improved exercise tolerance, and a reduced need for nitroglycerine and pain relievers. These results were published in peer-reviewed scientific journals. The patients included 283 with occlusive atherosclerotic vascular disease, with 87 percent showing improvements. This was despite the fact that minerals and trace elements depleted by the EDTA were not replaced, and risk factors (such as tobacco use) were not changed.

Dr. Clarke witnessed these miraculous recoveries and observed that, after chelation therapy, previously metal-contaminated tissues resumed normal function. He continued to be an avid proponent of chelation therapy and was largely responsible for generating scientific interest and keeping it alive during the first

20 years of its use. Dr. Clarke lived to be 92 years of age with a sharp mind and sustained interest in chelation therapy.

Other doctors, realizing the merits of chelation therapy, had begun extensive clinical treatment programs in private hospitals. One such physician was H. Ray Evers, M.D. He and his staff administered chelation therapy to 3,000 patients over a six-year period at Columbia General Hospital. Dr. Evers observed that "from our experience in treating …patients with varying degrees of calcinosis (arteriosclerosis, atherosclerosis, etc.), we will unequivocably state that it is our opinion that every patient with this disease in any part of the body should be given a therapeutic trial before any type of vascular surgery is performed."

He also noted: "We find…in all cases of angina, characterized by the patient having no need for vasodilators after about the fifth infusion…and that ninety-one percent of these problems in the lower extremities make significant gains, including regaining ability to walk long distances comfortably, freedom from claudication, and evidence of improved distal circulation."

1964—Alfred Soffer, M.D., associate in medicine at Northwestern University Medical School and former director of the Cardiopulmonary Laboratory of Rochester, New York, published his book "Chelation Therapy." In it, he pointed out that patients suffering from peripheral vascular disease, especially those with diabetes, seemed to benefit from regular EDTA chelation therapy.

Clinical trials testing EDTA's benefits to the cardiovascular system were conducted by H. Richard Casdorph, M.D., Ph.D., assistant clinical professor of medicine at the medical school at University of California, Irvine.

In his book *Bypassing Bypass Surgery*, Elmer M. Cranton, M.D., reports that "Dr. Casdorph, utilizing sophisticated new noninvasive radioactive isotopes, demonstrated a statistically significant improvement of heart function and a highly significant increase in blood flow to the brain in patients with atherosclerosis. Precise measurements of cardiac injection fraction (the percentage of blood pumped from the large chamber of the heart with each contraction) were determined before and after chelation therapy. Similar isotope techniques were used to confirm increased blood flow in carotid arteries and in the brain itself following chelation. The statistical probability that measured improvement could have been due to pure chance was less than one in ten thousand."

Other professionals engaged in similar studies included Drs. E. W. McDonagh, C.J. Randolph, and E. Cheraskin. The protocol consisted of measuring blood flow before and after EDTA chelation therapy, using the individual patients as their own controls. Dr. E.W. McDonagh and his colleagues used a unique brain blood flow study. They varied pressure on the eyeball to measure pressure of blood flow to the anterior of the eye. This is a valid test because the artery that promotes blood flow to the eye is connected to the carotid artery to the brain and blood pressure/flow within the eye corresponds to that in the brain.

Again, patients were used as their own controls, and their blood pressure flow measurements were taken before and after EDTA administration. Results were very impressive.

It is important to note that these two studies, performed independently of each other, followed scientific protocol and supported the effectiveness of chelation therapy. Scientists find more credence in studies when their results are independently validated by separate facilities and researchers.

More advances and accomplishments
In 1978, Dr. Evers, mentioned earlier was pulled into a legal battle to uphold the validation of chelation therapy. He won a court case that supported a doctor's right to use a drug approved for one condition by the FDA to treat another condition for which its used has not been approved. An excerpt from the docket (United States vs. Evers, 453 F. Supp. 141 Cal.Rptr 764, 774, [1970]) the court ruled in favor of Dr. Evers, stating that:

"To require prior State approval before advising – prescribing – administering – a new treatment modality for an informed consenting patient is to suppress innovation by the person best qualified to make medical progress. The treating doctor, the clinician, is at the cutting edge of medical knowledge.

"The mention of a requirement that licensed doctors must prescribe, treat, 'within State-sanctioned alternatives' raises the spector of medical stagnation at the best, statism, paternalist big brother at worst. It is by the alternatives to orthodoxy that medical

progress has been made. A free, progressive society has an enormous stake in recognizing and protecting this right of the physician...Irrespective of the strong medical school of thought that chelation has not been clinically shown to help arteriosclerosis, the weight of the evidence submitted to this court is to the contrary."

I knew Dr. Evers personally and he was a great influence in my life. In fact, I credit him for saving my life when I was 16 years old. I had collapsed from a heart infection from the coxsackie virus after a bout with mono and tonsillitis and was given very little hope of living. I was hospitalized and at one point in the coronary care unit, I had to be resuscitated. Through my grandfather, I met Dr. Evers who began treating me with chelation and became my friend and mentor. He even encouraged me to study medicine after I graduated from high school.

After the chelation treatments, I became stronger and healthier than ever. (In fact, as an adult, I passed the U.S. Air Force military flight physical). Dr. Evers brought not only physical wholeness, but emotional and spiritual wellness, too. He took me to church on Sundays. This was my first exposure to religion, since my parents didn't attend a church and my father was an agnostic.

Later, when I was a junior in college, Dr. Evers invited me to his home for dinner. While I was there I told him I had decided to become a doctor. I remember him asking me, "Why do you want to become a doctor? You've got to know your 'why.' "

I answered, "Because God told me to." He said, "Then I'll do everything I can to encourage you." (Until that time, I had planned on becoming a lawyer).

I credit God, Dr. Evers, and my father who was on the food science research team at Armour Foods, for placing me on the path I am on today. My father did research on fatty acids and took me to work with him when I was only four years old. I lived in the labs until I started kindergarten.

1979—Chelation expert Bruce W. Halstead, M.D. published a physician's treatise on chelation therapy: "The Scientific Basis of EDTA Chelation Therapy." Following is an excerpt from page 14 of that publication:

"*Experimentation and usage of EDTA chelation therapy has resulted in the development of techniques for the successful treatment of the catastrophic effects of atherosclerosis involving coronary artery disease, stroke, senility, early gangrene, essential hypertension, peripheral vascular occlusive disease, osteoarthritis, and related disorders…Clinical studies…have consistently shown a definite improvement in the circulation of the patient as evidenced by improvement in skin color, improvement of arterial pulsation in the feet, return of normal temperature to the feet, regaining ability to walk long distances comfortably, elimination of anginal pain, improved brain function and improvement of muscle coordination…Chelation therapy generally results in a significant improvement in coronary circulation, in most cases to the extent that the patient no longer requires the use of nitroglycerin or similar drugs…In a large number of cases, chelation therapy has been found to improve kidney function, decrease the amount of insulin required by diabetics, and produce significant improvement in arthritis and some cases of Parkinson's disease."*

1980—A clinical study in Switzerland revealed a 90 percent reduction in cancer in a group of 59 chelation patients (compared to 231 control patients) that were monitored over a 10-year period. The researchers contacted the patients again in 1989 and found that only 1 of the 59 treated patients had died of cancer, compared to 30 of the 172 control subjects who had died of the disease.

In that same year, Robert J. Rogers, M.D. won a Florida Court case upholding his right to administer chelation therapy for cardiovascular disease. The Supreme Court of Florida ruled that:

"…[We] affirm the result of the district court's decision because, under the particular facts of this case, it appears that the action of the Board of Medical Examiners restraining Dr. Rogers from further utilization of chelation treatment was an arbitrary and unreasonable exercise of the state's police power…The Board's findings do not support a conclusion of quackery…"

1980-1990s—Results of several clinical studies with chelation therapy were published in peer-reviewed medical journals by Edward W. McDonagh, Charles J. Rudolph, and Emanuel Cheaskin.

1993—In a Danish study, 65 patients waiting for bypass surgery for six months were treated with chelation therapy. Eighty-nine percent of these patients improved to the point that they canceled their surgery. In 27 patients, 24 affected limbs were saved from amputation.

The report, "Historical Perspectives on the Development of Chelation Therapies," states:

"Of 92 patients referred for surgical intervention, only 10 required surgery after or during their treatment period with chelation therapy. The savings amounted to $3,000,000 in insurance benefits. The study spanned a period of six years, with no severe side effects or deaths arising from the treatment. The authors concluded that EDTA chelation therapy is safe, effective, and cost-saving.

"L. Terry Chapell, in a letter to the editor of the Journal of Advancement in Medicine, noted that if similar results were obtained in the United States of America, in 1992 alone, 363,000 of 407,000 coronary artery bypasses would have been avoided and 102,000 limbs would have been saved with treatment by chelation therapy. The direct cost savings, in 1992 alone, could have been as much as $8,000,000,000. The only plausible explanations for Hancke's positive data are that not all surgery is necessary or that the EDTA treatment is highly effective—or both."

Today, chelation therapy continues to produce the same remarkable and life-giving results. Some of the conditions responding to chelation therapy include coronary artery disease, such as blockage of arteries in arms and legs and early gangrene. However, current therapy is employed with intravenous EDTA chelation. It has its drawbacks, including possible trace mineral depletion. Also, when large amounts of lead are removed quickly from the body by chelation or other means, the kidneys may be damaged.

Chelation therapy today

Chelation therapy has made terrific strides in the last few years. Oral chelation, using vitamins and other supplements, has risen in popularity. Now an exciting and revolutionary approach to chelation is available. Chelation has been "rediscovered" through a safe, yet powerful suppository modality. is my chelation suppository of choice because it has scientific proof of bioavailability and absorption superior to even that of IV chelation therapy. Formulated over nine years, Detoxamin® is a unique, patented and proprietary blend that no other suppository matches. Detoxamin is the original trusted and credible brand and that is why it is my choice.

It is exciting for me to be involved as the principal investigator in cutting-edge research of pharmacokinetic (absorption and bioavailability) studies, as well as prostate condition-specific clinical trials of Detoxamin. We are truly "rediscovering chelation "with a new and novel route of delivery and superior mechanism of action to intravenous treatment. The active ingredient, calcium disodium EDTA, circulates in the blood and is present in body tissues longer to do its chelating work.

Detoxamin's effectiveness is validated by the impressive health benefits I observe—not only in my patients, but with research study participants, as well.

(Although Detoxamin is powerful and effective when used alone, some people choose to combine it with intravenous chelation therapy and that's certainly an individual choice). Detoxamin is the easiest and fastest method of chelation and certainly fits in with today's "on the go" lifestyle. Where intravenous chelation takes hours of sitting in one spot (a real infringement on a person's time), Detoxamin works gently overnight, without side effects, and even children can use it. I will describe more about this groundbreaking medical and scientific advancement and my clinical experience with it later in this book.

References

1. Doll R, Fishbein L, Infante P, Landrigan P, Lloyd JW, Mason TJ, Mastromatteo E, Norseth T, et al. Problems of epidemiological evidence. *Environ. Health Perspect.* 1981;40:11-20.
2. Kazantzis G. Role of cobalt, iron, lead, manganese, mercury, platinum, selenium and titanium in carcinogenesis. *Environ/ Health Perspect.* 1981;40:143-161.
3. "Smaller power sources on the horizon" by Sandeep Junnakar. Nov. 13, 2002. [http://CNET News.com; 6/26/2007].
4. "Historical Perspectives on the Development of Chelation Therapies." An Extended Compendium Prepared for the Advanced Training Seminar on Heavy Metal Toxicology. September 1998. Sponsored by the Great Lakes College of Medicine. Prepared by John Parks Trowbridge MD, FACAM, Diplomate ABCT. Permission granted to Life Center Houston to publish on the healthCHOICESnow.com website.

Chapter III
Testing for Heavy Metals:
Eliminate the Bad and Ugly

Human beings have been exposed to toxic heavy metals for thousands of years. Even the ancient Roman civilization wasn't exempt. Today we are inundated with these insidious contaminants more than ever in history. Modern industrial and commercial practices pollute our drinking water, air and soil with toxic metal compounds. These harmful metals are involved in mining and the manufacture of consumer goods, as well as burning and refining processes. Toxic heavy metals are found in a vast array of sources: construction materials, cosmetics, medicines and fuels, to name just a few. They infiltrate your daily life through common everyday commodities such as baking powder, personal care products, pesticides, and antibiotics. Although there are more than 20 different metal toxins that can harm you, I will concentrate on the five most prevalent ones: mercury, lead, aluminum, cadmium and arsenic. As I review them and the detrimental impact they have on your health, it's interesting to note that some of the diseases related to toxic metal poisoning have the same symptoms as the poisonings themselves. For instance, compare the symptoms of multiple sclerosis, autism and mercury poisoning:

<u>Chronic Mercury Poisoning Symptoms</u>
- anxiety/nervousness, often with difficulty in breathing
- irritability
- restlessness

- exaggerated response to stimulation
- fearfulness
- emotional instability - lack of self control
  -fits of anger, with violent, irrational behavior
- loss of self confidence
- indecision
- shyness or timidity, being easily embarrassed
- loss of memory
- inability to concentrate
- lethargy/drowsiness
- insomnia
- mental depression, despondency
- withdrawal
- suicidal tendencies
- manic depression
- numbness and tingling of hands, feet, fingers, toes, or lips
- muscle weakness progressing to paralysis
- ataxia
- tremors/trembling of hands, feet, lips, eyelids or tongue
- lack of coordination

MS Symptoms
- blurred vision or double vision (diplopia)
- loss of vision in one eye
- paresthesia or pain
- numbness or tingling
- weakness in an arm or leg
- feeling heavy
- loss of strength anywhere in the body
- dizziness or vertigo
- tightness around the chest
- poor balance or staggering
- development of a limp or dragging foot
- seizures
- tremors

- spasticity
- headaches
- cognitive impairments
- depression
- fatigue
- slurred speech
- bladder or bowel problems

Autism Symptoms

- shyness, social withdrawal
- anxiety, irrational fears
- irritability
- aggression
- temper tantrums
- loss of speech
- delayed language
- over-sensitivity to light
- blurred vision
- circling, rocking, toe walking
- abnormal gait and posture
- clumsiness and lack of coordination
- difficulties sitting, lying, crawling and walking
- poor concentration and attention
- poor short-term memory
- poor visual and perceptual motor skills
- agitation
- insomnia
- abnormal touch sensations, touch aversion
- decreased muscle strength
- poor appetite

Lead

Mined extensively in Missouri, Colorado, Idaho and Utah, lead is the fifth most utilized heavy metal in the United States. Lead is one of the most harmful elements on Earth and is absorbed into the body following inhalation or ingestion. Exposure to lead can come from a myriad of sources, including drinking water and airborne lead particulates. It is widely recognized as a neurotoxin and high concentrations can cause irreversible brain damage. Lead can kill brain cells, causing seizure, coma, and even death. Excessive blood lead levels in children can cause learning disabilities, attention deficit disorder, hyperactivity and intelligence reduction. Note: Antimony, often alloyed with lead, is also toxic.

Sources of exposure: air pollution, batteries, cast iron products, canned foods, ceramics, chemical fertilizers, cosmetics, dolomite, dust, foods grown in industrial zones, gasoline, black hair dyes and rinses, mascara, leaded glass, newsprint and color advertisements, paints, pesticides, pewter, pottery, rubber toys, soft coal, soil, solder, putty, tap water, tobacco smoke, vinyl products.

Symptoms of lead poisoning: Abdominal pain, anemia, anorexia, anxiety, bone pain, brain damage, confusion, constipation, convulsions, diminished motor reaction times, dizziness, drowsiness, fatigue, headaches, hypertension, inability to concentrate, indigestion, irritability, appetite loss, muscle incoordination, memory problems, miscarriage, muscle pain, tremors, vomiting, weakness.

Target tissues/organs: Bones, brain, heart, kidneys, liver, nervous system, pancreas.

Disease links: Dementia, brain cancer, high blood pressure, kidney failure, cardiovascular disease, liver impairment, myocardial infarction, stroke, birth defects.

Arsenic

Not only is arsenic famous in detective novels and screenplays as the secret poison of choice, arsenic is the most common environmental cause of heavy metal toxicity in humans. It enters the environment through volcanic gas and ash, and can also enter the environment when volcanic rocks are eroded by running water. It is an industrial byproduct of metal smelting processes, and can enter the atmosphere as arsine gas or enter the water supply in effluent. People can also be exposed to arsenic through common household products such as paints and wood preservatives. Perhaps the most prevalent sources are pesticides and fungicides used both around the house and in agriculture. Arsenic can cause damage to the peripheral nervous system, leading to numbness in the hands and feet, tingling, and feeling "pins and needles." It can appear as a darkening of the skin (not due to exposure to sunlight). Excessive exposure can also appear as white bands in the fingernails a month or more after a critical dosing, as well as excessive growth of the skin on the palms and soles of the feet. Arsenic inhibits the cellular uptake of glucose and interferes with fatty acid oxidation and production of coenzyme A. It also blocks the production of glutathione which prevents oxidative cell damage. Arsenic can also interfere with normal enzyme activity, and may be linked to direct damage of DNA. Arsenic is also indicated in liver damage and is probably carcinogenic.

Sources of exposure: Pesticides, fungicides, water supply, volcanic discharge, metal smelting, paints and wood preservatives, colored chalk and household detergents.

Symptoms of arsenic poisoning: Acute symptoms include rawness of the throat from ingestion/breathing, red skin or rash at point of contact, severe abdominal pain and vomiting and diarrhea. Chronic exposure can lead to anorexia, fever, inflammation of the mucosal membranes, heart arrhythmia, liver damage and jaundice, and gangrene.

Target tissues/organs: Red blood cells, central nervous system, kidneys, liver, skin, and digestive tract.

Disease links: Anorexia, multiple cancers, bronchitis, emphysema, diabetes mellitus, heart attack, liver cirrhosis, stillbirths and postneonatal mortality, blackfoot disease.

Iron

It may come as a surprise to find iron on the list of toxic heavy metals. It is, after all, essential to our bodies as a trace nutrient to maintain healthy blood. However, our environment does not contain substantial amounts of iron, and evolution has designed our bodies to retain as much iron as possible. In fact, the human body does not have an excretory pathway for iron. Thus, the human body is completely defenseless against excessive exposure to iron. Acute iron poisoning can manifest as nausea and diarrhea, sometimes with blood loss. Scarring of the digestive tract can occur. Elevated blood glucose levels are observed. Chronic symptoms include cirrhosis of the liver, amenorrhea (loss of period) in women, and impotence in men. A dose as small as 3 grams, can lead to severe poisoning in toddlers. It may come as even more of a surprise that the most common source of iron poisoning is over-the-counter prenatal vitamins and iron supplements. Exposure to iron and certain pesticides may be linked to Parkinson's disease.

Sources of exposure: High-dose iron supplements, prenatal vitamins with high-dose iron.

Symptoms of iron poisoning: Severe vomiting, diarrhea, abdominal pain, dehydration, lethargy, bloody stool. Acute symptoms may disappear, but the toxicity will spread to other organs and will have chronic effects unless confronted. Iron can also be accumulated to toxic levels without manifesting acute symptoms.

Target tissues/organs: Liver, gastrointestinal organs, kidneys, heart, brain, spleen, adrenal glands, thymus gland.

Disease links: Hemachromatosis (iron accumulation in organs), cirrhosis of the liver, amenorrhea, impotence, gastrointestinal damage, Parkinson's Disease.

Mercury

Mercury is everywhere in today's world: it not only degasses from the earth's crust in volcanic emissions and evaporates from bodies of water; it also comes from commercial processes like burning fossil fuels (such as coal), incinerating waste, forest fires, fertilizers, and fungicides. Mercury accumulates in the body and has been implicated in neurological disorders such as multiple sclerosis and Lou Gehrig's disease. Occupations that chronically expose workers to mercury include dentistry, painting, electrical, pharmaceutical and laboratory, farming, factory production, mining, chemistry and beautician work.

Sources of exposure: Thermometers, barometers, fluorescent light bulbs, pesticides, fungicides, dental fillings, vaccines (thimerosal is still in vaccines in thresholds considered un-reportable), skin-tightening creams, antiseptic creams, laxatives, diuretics, mercurochrome antiseptic, skin lightening creams, psoriasis creams, some waxes and polishes.

Symptoms of mercury poisoning: Abdominal pain, vomiting, diarrhea, hemorrhage, chronic bronchitis, lung problems, kidney disorders, fatigue, insomnia, loss of memory, excitability, chest pains, reduction of sensory and motor nerve function, depression, visual and/or auditory hallucinations, muscular tremors, sleep disorders, alterations in heart rate, blood pressure and automatic reflexes, impaired coordination, speech disorders, dementia, headaches, senility, and diminished mental function.

<u>Target tissues/organs</u>: Central nervous system, gastrointestinal system, kidneys, liver.

<u>Disease links</u>: Multiple sclerosis, autism, cerebral palsy, amyotrophic lateral sclerosis, Parkinson's disease, psychosis, chronic fatigue syndrome.

Cadmium

Since cadmium is found in zinc-, lead-, and copper-containing ores, industrial activities such as mining, smelting and refining metal ores discharge significant amounts of cadmium into the atmosphere. Fossil fuel burning, waste incineration and steel production also contribute their share, as do vented nickel-cadmium (Ni-Cad) batteries used in aircraft, buses, and diesel locomotives. And smokers beware: About 40 to 60 percent of cadmium inhaled through cigarette smoke is absorbed by the body as opposed to the five to 10 percent taken up from food or water. From all combined sources, it is estimated that 4,000 to 13,000 tons of cadmium are released annually into the environment.

<u>Sources of exposure</u>: Nickel-cadmium batteries, PVC plastics, paint pigments, bone meal, insecticides, fungicides, phosphate fertilizers, cigarettes, dental amalgams, electroplating, motor oil, exhaust, food grown in cadmium-laden soil, meats (kidneys, liver, poultry), power plants, seafood (crab, flounder, mussels, oysters, scallops), fresh-water fish, "softened" water, smelting plants, welding fumes, cigarette smoke, coffee, tea, colas and refined cereals.

<u>Symptoms of cadmium poisoning</u>: Anemia, dry and scaly skin, emphysema, fatigue, hair loss, heart disease, depressed immune response, hypertension, joint pain, kidney stones, liver dysfunction, loss of appetite, diminished sense of smell, lung cancer, pain in the back and legs, yellow teeth.

<u>Target tissues/organs</u>: Appetite, and pain centers in the brain, liver, placenta, kidneys, lungs, bones, cardiovascular system.

<u>Disease links</u>: Immune system deficiencies, lung cancer, prostate problems, birth defects and miscarriage, behavioral and learning disabilities.

Aluminum

Even though it technically is not considered a "heavy" metal, aluminum is a toxic metal and the third most abundant element on earth. Besides a myriad of commercial sources, aluminum comes to us from out of the sky and land. Acid rain—originating from air pollution—comes into contact with soil and other sources, to dissolve aluminum compounds and spread them widely over the planet. Some scientists and health professionals believe that bioaccumulation of aluminum could be responsible for at least ten common neurological disorders—including Alzheimer's disease, Parkinson's disease and senile and pre-senile dementia. Note: Beryllium, a metal in some ways similar to aluminum and used in exotic aircraft and spacecraft parts, as well as bicycle wheels, is also toxic.

Sources of exposure: Cookware, aluminum foil, baking powder, alum, vanilla powder, beer, dental cements and amalgams, dentures, toothpaste, antacids, antiperspirants, buffered aspirin, nasal spray, prescription and over-the-counter medications for diarrhea, hemorrhoids, vaginal cleansing products, cigarette filters, city drinking water, automotive exhaust, leather tanning products, appliances and building materials.

Symptoms of aluminum poisoning: Excessive headaches, abnormal heart rhythm, depression, numbness in the hands and feet, blurred vision, muscle pain, psychosis, fatigue, long-term memory impairment, psychomotor speed, loss of balance, inability to pronounce words properly, even liver and kidney failure.

Target tissues/organs: brain, muscles, liver, lungs, bones, kidneys, skin, reproductive system, and stomach.

Disease links: Alzheimer's disease; dementia; anemia; Parkinson's disease; Amyotrophic lateral sclerosis (ALS or Lou Gehrig's disease); birth defects.

Nickel

Nickel is a heavy metal used in the automobile industry, electronics, as a catalyst in chemical processes, in nickel-cadmium batteries, many household products and in cheap jewelry. Environmental nickel comes from surface runoff, industrial and municipal waste discharges, and natural erosion from soil and rocks. You can become allergic from contact with nickel jewelry.

The nickel ions are transported through the sweat into the skin. Nickel can cause cancer of the upper respiratory tract and it is thought that its carcinogenic effects are due to its lipid-peroxidation properties that burn the cell's fatty membrane, causing DNA-strand gaps and breaks and DNA-protein crosslinks. Foods like cocoa, soybeans, some dried legumes and nuts, and oatmeal contain high concentrations of nickel.

Sources of exposure: Cigarette smoke, air pollution, burning fossil fuels, mining and refining operations, fertilizers, incineration of municipal waste, soil treated with sewage sludge, electroplating industry, drinking water, baking powder, hydrogenated fats and oils, dental work and stainless steel cookware.

Symptoms of nickel poisoning: rhinitis, sinusitis, nasal septal perforation, asthma, dermatitis, kidney damage, headaches, vertigo, nausea, vomiting, insomnia.

Target tissues/organs: respiratory system, gastrointestinal system, urinary system, immune system, skin.

Disease links: Lung and nasal cancers.

Other Toxic Heavy Metals

There are approximately 35 "heavy metals", of which 23 are listed as being toxic to humans. A heavy metal is defined as having a density 5 times greater than water. Technology has introduced uses for heavy metals that have never before been present in our environment, and hence new avenues for humans to be exposed to those heavy metals. Many metals that are not present in the environment at substantial levels have been introduced for medical uses. For instance, barium is used as a medical diagnostic. Barium is not excessively toxic, however it can displace potassium and cause decrease in muscle tone, heart functioning and have effects on the nervous system. Barium is intentionally ingested for diagnosis using x-rays. Other heavy metals that can cause cumulative damage are bismuth and bromine. Many drugs, primarily for the treatment of digestive problems of the stomach, such as Pepto-Bismol, contain bismuth or bromine.

Other heavy metals that are found at trace levels in the environment simply cannot be tolerated by the human body. One example is thallium. Chronic effects include problems with the kidneys, heart, respiratory and nervous system. Severe neuritis can result causing fatigue and weight loss, sometimes so severe that it can be crippling. In addition, thallium can cross the placental barrier and affect unborn children. Thallium, like mercury, is used in some thermometers; thallium, like arsenic, is used to intentionally poison people. Heavy metals such as uranium and plutonium can have a direct effect on producing cancer through radioactivity. These metals have been liberated into the atmosphere by atomic testing and nuclear power accidents.

We do not have the time or space to discuss all 23 toxic heavy metals- even titanium, platinum, and "cheap gold" used in jewelry can elicit skin reactions and possibly other symptoms in humans. However, each of these heavy metals can be detected by clinical tests of the urine or blood to evaluate your initial toxic burden.

Cancers Associated with Heavy Metals

Toxic Metal	Type of Cancer
Arsenic	Skin, Lung, Bladder, Kidney, Liver, Prostate
Mercury	Liver, Esophageal, Lung, Prostate
Aluminum	Bladder, Kidney, Brain
Nickel	Lung, nasal
Cadmium	Prostate
Uranium	Lung
Tungsten	Lung
Antimony	Lung
Beryllium	Lung

Diagnostic Recommendations for Heavy Metal Toxicity

The most common types of tests are listed below; however, please note that urine and feces samples offer the most accurate methods for diagnosing individual toxic heavy metal burden. It's important that you take a test for heavy metals both before *and* after undergoing a chelation regimen. That way you can assess your levels and monitor your progress.

Fecal Metals

Analysis of elements in feces provides important information about the potential for toxic metal burden. For many heavy metals, fecal (biliary) excretion is the primary natural route of elimination from the body. The efficiency of oral absorption of toxic metals varies considerably; therefore, fecal elemental analysis also provides a direct indication of dietary exposure. Specimen collection is convenient for you and only requires a single-step procedure.

Urine Elements

Analyzing elements in urine provides valuable information on potentially toxic elements such as lead, mercury, cadmium, nickel, arsenic and aluminum, and measures the efficiency of the kidney's ability to resorb essential minerals such as magnesium, calcium, sodium and potassium.

Hair Elements

Extensive research has established that heavy metal levels in scalp hair are linked to levels throughout the entire body. For this reason, many researchers consider hair as the tissue of choice for analyzing toxins, as well as several nutritional elements. Unlike blood, hair element levels are not affected by daily fluctuations in toxicity. This is why deviations in hair element levels often appear prior to other more chronic symptoms and can act as a beneficial and early predictor for later health problems. Please note: the hair elements test works for healthy people, but the hair protein productions of ill people are unreliable. My sickest patients have low to no levels of these elements because their bodies cannot make protein for their hair.

<u>Red Blood Cell Elements</u> (*this test can only be performed by a physician*)

Analysis of red blood cells provides the best diagnostic tool for assessing the status of elements that have important functions inside cells or on blood cell membranes. Blood cell element levels are useful for assessing cardiac influences, anti-inflammatory processes, anemia, immunological function, glucose tolerance and other disorders that are associated specifically with zinc deficiency.

Red blood cell (RBC) analysis is an invaluable diagnostic method for assessing insufficiency or excess of elements that have important functions within cells or on blood cell membranes. An important feature is that the cells are not washed, because this would result in partial loss of some important elements that bind to the plasma membrane—for example, calcium.

Tests/Assessments Information

All laboratory test kits for the presence of heavy metals are available in postage-paid self-contained mailers for easy-to-use home specimen collection (except for the RBC test, which requires blood drawn by a physician).

In the next chapter, I discuss the various types of chelation treatments currently available, as well as examine their efficacies. It is important that you understand the scope of chelation programs and what they have to offer you and your health.

References

1. "Detoxify or Die." Sherry A. Rogers, MD. Sand Key Company, Inc. Sarasota, FL. 2002.
2. Multiple Sclerosis Symptoms. (National Multiple Sclerosis Society).
3. Bernard S, Enayati A, Binstock T, Roger H, Redwood L, McGinnis W. Autism: A Unique Type of Mercury Poisoning. ARC Research. April, 2000.
4. "Detoxify or Die." Sherry A. Rogers, MD. Sand Key Company, Inc. Sarasota, FL. 2002.
5. Ibid.
6. Dartmouth Toxic Metal Research Program. (A program of the Center for Environmental Health Sciences at Dartmouth). Report: Dartmouth Toxic Metals Research Program: The facts on cadmium.
7. Oral Chelation and Nutritional Replacement Therapy for Chemical & Heavy Metal Toxicity and Cardiovascular Disease by Maile Pouls, Ph.D. (Townsend Letter, 1999).
8. "Detoxify or Die." Sherry A. Rogers, MD. Sand Key Company, Inc. Sarasota, FL. 2002.
9. Nickel, nickel carbonyl, and some nickel compounds Health and Safety Guide. World Health Organization, Geneva 1991.
10. Steven Marcus, MD, Professor, Department of Preventive Medicine and Community Health, Associate Professor, Department of Pediatrics, New Jersey Medical School, University of Medicine and Dentistry of New Jersey; Executive and Medical Director, New Jersey Poison Information and Education System; Consulting Staff, Departments of Pediatrics and Internal Medicine, University Hospital, University of Medicine and Dentistry of New Jersey; Consulting Staff, Department of Pediatrics, Newark Beth Israel Medical Centerhttp://www.emedicine.com/emerg/topic42.htm : Toxicity, Arsenic
11. Clifford Spanierman, MD, Consulting Staff, Departments of Emergency Medicine and Pediatrics, Lutheran General Hospital of Oak Brook, Advocate Health System: http://www.emedicine.com/emerg/topic285.htm " Toxicity, Iron"

Chapter IV
The Toxic Metal Connection to Major Diseases

Some metals are classified as important micronutrients. Examples include iron, manganese, chromium, cobalt, copper, selenium, zinc, and vanadium. However, the body needs them only in very small amounts and they can become toxic when ingested in excessive quantities. This is because these metals are in a "free form," meaning they are not bound in a protein-bound (chelated) state. Please note: all non-menstruating women should check their multi-mineral/vitamin formulas for iron content, as this mineral is not needed in your supplement after menopause. The same holds true for men because iron can build up to toxic levels in the body.

Metals that are ALWAYS toxic and should never be ingested include the following: mercury, antimony, arsenic, beryllium, bismuth, cadmium, copper, lead, nickel, platinum, thallium, tungsten, uranium, and aluminum. Diagnostic imaging dyes containing ingredients such as barium, bismuth and thallium are a common source of heavy metal contamination.

Once the body is poisoned by heavy metals, cells can be harmed or even killed by their resulting generation of free radicals (called reactive oxygen species or ROS). These errant molecules, which I measure in my patient population, can injure the lipid-rich membrane of the cell membrane in a process known as "lipid peroxidation." Once inside the cell, free radicals can harm the nuclear lipid cell membrane and infiltrate the cell's replication mechanisms (DNA). This action can damage the cell membrane and potentially initiate the cancer-causing process. Metals can bond to cell membranes, producing complexes or "ligands" that essentially paralyze the cell from performing its daily tasks and can falsely integrate into the cell membrane structure. This process leads to malfunction or even death of the affected cell. Metals primarily inactivate certain enzyme systems or degrade the structure of key enzyme proteins—forever rendering them useless—and this is how metals damage the human body. This is like shutting down all avenues of mass transit in a city. Enzymes act as messengers for the vasodilating mechanisms and are metal ion cofactor dependent. Get the wrong metals in there and your blood vessels will not dilate. Also, metals like mercury, cadmium and nickel deplete the body's normal antioxidant mechanisms responsible for neutralizing free radical activity.

Research shows that metals can activate signaling of genes responsible for triggering cancerous conditions in the body, including the P53 gene linked to breast cancer.

Symptoms of metal toxicity in the body can include:

- Brain disease
- Lowered IQ
- Kidney damage
- Diminished immune system function
- Cardiovascular problems
- Bone and soft tissue disease
- Fungal infections
- Thyroid and other glandular imbalances

- Cognitive disorders: ADHD, Alzheimer's disease, depression, etc.
- Unrelenting fatigue

All of these symptoms are manifestations of damage to the body, starting at the cellular level. As examples, I have examined the link of heavy metal toxicity to the following current major health concerns.

Cancer

Lead is one of the most pervasive toxic metals on the planet. It exists in the soil from decades of lead-based auto exhaust emissions and crumbling dust from older structures painted with lead paint. When tracked inside, vacuuming can even kick up lead particles into the air. You don't need acute toxicity of lead to cause problems. As I mentioned before, research shows that even LOW lead levels are linked to our two greatest causes of death: cancer and heart disease. Global chronic low-level metal toxicity is recognized as a problem by such notable agencies as the U.S. Environmental Protection Agency (EPA), U.S. Food and Drug Administration (FDA), and Centers for Disease Control (CDC), as well as local health departments. What is really scary is that lead levels formerly accepted as tolerable by government monitoring agencies have been adjusted lower and lower since the 1960s, as these agencies realize that even low levels do tremendous harm.

Currently, accepted lead levels in blood are 30 micrograms per deciliter. However, I believe the only safe level is no level. All the patients I've randomly screened have three to four metals present. This means we are all at risk, since today nearly one in three people come down with cardiovascular disease and one out of two come down with cancer. I believe there is definitely a toxic metal connection to these chronic diseases. What if every patient I randomly screened was positive for three to four disease-causing bacteria in their systems? No competent physician would accept that finding without further investigation. We would never ignore three to four bacteria, so why would we ignore three to four toxic metals?

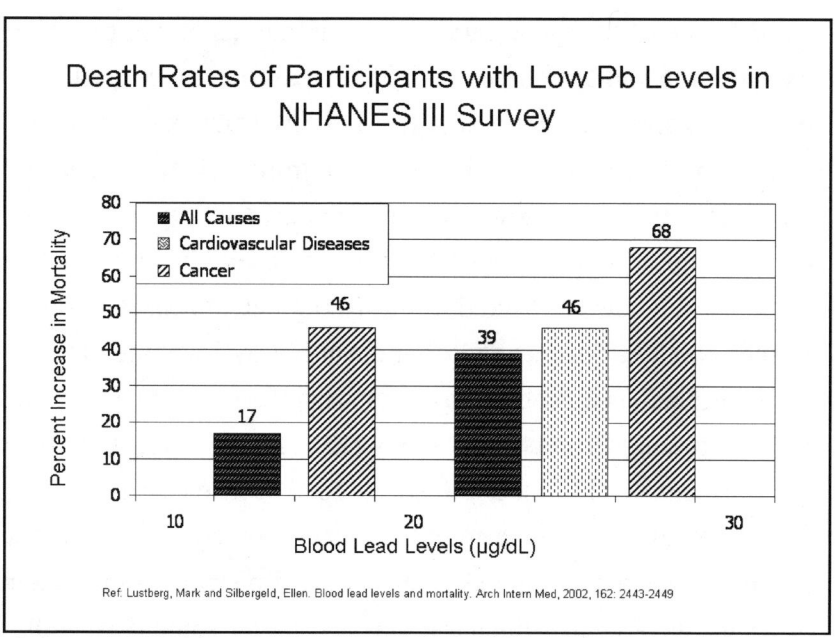

Workers in lead-associated occupations are twice as likely to die from brain cancer than people in other industries. This is according to a study conducted by the University of Rochester Medical Center. Before the results of this study were released, scientists thought that the major risk factor for brain cancer was radiation exposure. The new data was based on information from the U.S. Census Bureau and the National Death Index and published in the Sept. 1, 2006, issue of the *International Journal of Cancer.* The study involved a census sample of 317,968 people who reported their occupations between 1979 and 1981. Targeted in the survey were gas station attendants from the 1970s and early 1980s, painters, automobile mechanics, firefighters, engineers, automobile assemblers, truck drivers, plumbers, welders, and workers in the printing industries. When study author Edwin van Wijingaarden, Ph.D. tracked their cancer rates for nine years, he found that the death rate among workers whose jobs exposed them to lead was 50 percent higher than unexposed people.

Alzheimer's disease

Alzheimer's disease is a serious ailment, marked by an initial decline in memory and then progressing to personality changes, deterioration of mental functioning and sometimes even aggressive or irrational behavior. In effect, Alzheimer's disease ruins brains and damages families. Free radical-induced oxidative stress—as well as abnormal protein metabolism—have been linked to this disorder, starting with injury to the brain's nerve cell membranes. Through a series of oxidative stress pathways, aluminum, lead, and other metals can cause normal brain proteins to aggregate or fuse to each other and cause the "neurofibrillary tangle formations" characteristic of Alzheimer's disease. Aluminum is a major metal implicated in this disorder and is found in fluoridated drinking water, deodorants, cookware, antacids, baking powder and cosmetics.

Lead is connected to deterioration in the brain and could very well be implicated in Alzheimer's disease. Don't forget that lead toxicity has already been well established, in that children exposed to lead are more vulnerable to lower IQs and aggressive behavior. A paper presented at the American Academy of Neurology meeting (May 2000) at Case Western University Medical School in Ohio supported the theory that occupations involving lead exposed their workers to more than twice as much risk of Alzheimer's, when compared to the average population. Jobs involved those connected to lead (including lead smelters and manufacturing of lead-containing batteries, pottery, pipes, and ammunition).

How about other metals like cadmium and arsenic? What could be the compounding effects of multiple metals, along with lead? Even though leaded gasoline and indoor lead-based paints have been phased out, millions of children are still at risk from sources. Lead can still be found in:

- Herbs that are lead-contaminated from foreign sources to increase their sale weights (primarily making adults sick)
- Toys from China (primarily making children sick)
- Older homes in the city, country, or suburbs, apartments, single-family homes, and both private and public housing
- Soil around a home that can attract lead from exterior paint or be contaminated from past use of leaded gas in cars.)
- Household dust contaminated from deteriorating lead-based paint/soil tracked into the home.
- Drinking water from plumbing with lead or lead solder.
- Lead-associated occupations can contaminate hands/clothes.

- Older painted toys and furniture and even some modern toy jewelry and embroidered baby bibs have been found to contain lead.
- Food and liquids stored in lead crystal or lead-glazed pottery or porcelain.
- Lead smelters or other industries that release lead into the air.
- Hobbies involving making pottery or stained glass, or refinishing furniture.

When children become adults, the lead doesn't just "go away." Once lead is in the body (via the digestive tract or respiratory system or absorbed through the skin) it is deposited in the bones, where we know it is stored. And bone lead stores increase as a person ages. When the body puts lead and other metals in bones, it displaces calcium, causing osteoporosis. By denying proper calcium uptake 1,000-fold, we get even more lead in our bones, causing a vicious cycle. Something tells me that this matters!

Lead poisoning in adults has been linked to high blood pressure, kidney failure and Alzheimer's disease. Ferid Murad and two other research colleagues were awarded the 1998 Nobel Prize in Physiology for their pioneering work in the 1980s that found nitric oxide to be a signaling molecule in the cardiovascular system that relaxes blood vessels.

Lead can cause erectile dysfunction (ED) by damaging the nitric oxide synthetase enzyme. This impairs the blood vessels' production of nitric oxide, a natural biochemical that opens up blood vessels (a process known as vasodilation) to promote proper circulation. So men experiencing ED would be better off having their heavy metal load tested rather than compounding the issue by taking drugs with side effects, like Viagra®. So why use a drug when you can be ready any time with healthy enzymes to produce nitric oxide yourself? I suggest you "get the lead out."

Coronary artery (cardiovascular) disease
Coronary artery disease (CAD) is the leading cause of death among American men and women. Risk factors include high blood pressure, physical inactivity, high cholesterol, smoking, obesity, and age. Now research also links heavy metal exposure to the list.

Coronary artery disease starts with changes in the tissue lining the blood vessels themselves. Heavy metal ions have been implicated in this process. For instance, researchers have discovered connections between iron stores, impaired nitric oxide pathways and cardiovascular problems. Just like lead, free-form iron can cause lipid peroxidation, oxidative stress, and endothelial cell membrane damage of the largest to the smallest vessel walls. This affects the action/production of endothelium-derived nitric oxide which—like lead—can cause problems like high blood pressure and erectile dysfunction.

I have found that whether you suffer from heart disease symptoms or any fatiguing illness, the common denominator is impairment of oxygen transport and cell waste removal. When fragile capillaries get "dinged" by oxidative stress, it starts this process. The key is to stop cell membrane injury. Once this is in place, you can improve blood flow and with improved circulation—and vital nutrition to repair the cell membrane—you can start to reverse or slow down any disease process. You need a healthy capillary to get to the tiniest cell, so anything that opens up and removes the metals causing poor blood flow can only serve to improve this circulation.

Multiple sclerosis

Multiple sclerosis (MS) is a disorder affecting the nervous system and impairs a person's ability to move, feel, and control his or her body functions. Nerve cells (neurons) "talk" to each other by way of electrical messages. These messages are channeled through the cells in an orderly manner because a thin layer of tissue called myelin acts as an insulator.

Mercury may provoke abnormal behavior by immune cells. When the myelin that sheathes neurons in the brain and spinal cord is attacked by the body's immune system, it damages this protective myelin cover. This slows the passages of electrical impulses through the neurons and, eventually, scar tissue or plaque (also called sclerosis) forms around the injured myelin. This condition interrupts cellular signals that control muscle coordination, strength, sensation, balance, and vision.

Affecting more than 250,000 people in the United States, MS hits people in their prime, usually between the ages of twenty and forty.

The mercury link

Mercury has been implicated in both mental and physical conditions in MS patients. A study comparing the mental health condition of 47 multiple sclerosis patients with mercury amalgams fillings to that of 50 patients with their fillings removed found that the subjects with amalgam fillings had many more challenges. When answers to the Beck Depression Inventory were tallied, it showed that MS patients with amalgams suffered significantly more depression. Their scores on the State-Trait Anger Expression Inventory showed they also experienced more anger. Another survey, called the SCL-90 Revised, revealed that those individuals with MS who still had mercury amalgam fillings suffered more symptoms of depression, and hostility—as well as psychotic and obsessive-compulsive behavior—than subjects who had had their amalgams removed.

Additionally, the MS subjects with amalgam fillings reported 43 percent more adverse health symptoms than those without amalgam fillings during that past year. Researchers deduced that the negative mental health symptoms exhibited by those MS patients with amalgams may be linked to the mercury in their fillings.

MS subjects with amalgams also exhibited significantly lower levels of red blood cells, hemoglobin and hematocrit when compared to MS subjects without amalgam fillings.

This condition greatly lowers transport of oxygen to cells. Thyroxine (a thyroid hormone) levels were also diminished in the amalgam group, as were total T lymphocytes and T-8 (CD8) suppressor cells, which make up a vital part of the immune system's defenses. Blood urea nitrogen levels were higher (indicating impaired kidney function) and serum IgG levels were diminished (a sign of weakened immune cell response). Further investigation indicates that mercury could actually cause the pathological and physiological changes characteristic of multiple sclerosis.

Note: The FDA recently came to a settlement with Moms Against Mercury in a lawsuit regarding amalgam fillings. The FDA's new view, posted on their Web site, now reads: "Dental amalgams contain mercury, which may have neurotoxic effects on the nervous systems of developing children and fetuses. When amalgam fillings are placed in teeth or removed from teeth, they release mercury vapor. Mercury vapor is also released during chewing." Read the statement in its entirety at http://www.fda.gov/cdrh/consumer/amalgams.html.

Facts About Mercury Toxicity

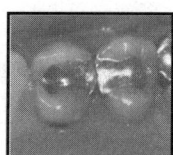

- ## Mercury Vapor
  - Most toxic
    - 100% absorbed at low dose
    - 74% absorbed at higher levels
  - Accumulates in critical organs*
    - Brain
    - Kidney
    - Transfers across the placental membrane into the fetus

Besides the disorders already covered in this chapter, I have found that heavy metals and their pathways of destruction, resulting in diminished blood flow, are linked to such diverse conditions such as autism, Parkinson's disease, chronic fatigue syndrome, fibromyalgia, sterility, infertility, benign prostatic hyperplasia (BPH), kidney dysfunction, and liver problems…just to name a few.

Remove, repair, revitalize
Heavy metals cause a domino effect: a chain reaction of metabolic events occurs, initiated by the presence of a heavy metal. When internal free radicals from heavy metals damage the cell's ability to excrete wastes, the cell can literally die in its own wastes. Then when the cell dies, it adds to the mix of free radicals.

Since poisoning of the cell and destruction of its life forces are the genesis of disease, and since cells make up tissues, tissues make up organs and organs comprise our body systems, it makes sense to start the healing pathway with the cell. As I mentioned before, if you can open the smallest capillary to reach the cell membrane of your deepest cell, I feel you can reverse the trend of disease and point your body toward abundant health. Detoxamin treatment improves circulation by removing toxic metals, thus preserving the enzyme action of nitric oxide synthetase. This Detoxamin treatment should be followed up with high quality nutrition.

In my practice, I have found that all conditions respond to the simple process I call "remove, repair and revitalize." In this book, I explain my total program that embraces this simple—yet profound—three-part approach to health and wellness.

References

1. Chen F, Shi X. "Intracellular signal transduction of cells in response to carcinogenic metals." *Crit. Rev. Oncol. Hematol.* 2002 Apr;42(1):105-21.

2. Wang Suwei, Shi Xianglin. "Mechanisms of 'Cr(VI)-induced p53 activation: the role of phosphorylation, mdm2 and ERK." Carcinogenesis. Vol. 22, No. 5. pp. 757-762, 2001.

3. Doll R, Fishbein L, Infante P, Landrigan P, Lloyd JW, Mason TJ, Mastromatteo E, Norseth T et al. Problems of epidemiological evidence. *Environ. Health Perspect.* 1981;40:11-20.

4. Kazantzis G. Role of cobalt, iron, lead, manganese, mercury, platinum, selenium and titanium in carcinogenesis. *Environ. Health Perspect.* 1981;40:143-161.

5. Toxic Heavy Metals: Sources and Specific Effects. (www.extremehealthusa.com).

6. Heavy Metal Toxicity. Life Extension. (www.lef.org/protocols/prtcls-txt/t-prtcl-156.htm).

7. Weyermann M, Brenner H. Factors Affecting Bone Demineralization and Blood Lead Levels of Postmenopausal Women—A Population-Based Study from Germany. *Environ. Res.* 1998; 76 (1):99-25(7).

8. Grizzo LT, Cordellini S. Perinatal Lead Exposure Affects Nitric Oxide and Cycloxygenase Pathways in Aorta. *Toxicol. Sci.* 2008; 103:207-214.

9. Siblerud et al. Evidence that mercury from silver dental fillings may be an etiological factor in multiple sclerosis. *Science of the Total Environment,* 1994 Mar 15.

10. Vimy M. Hahn LJ. Klober R. Takahashi Y. Lorscheider FL. Mercury uptake in sheep fetus from dental fillings, 32nd Annual Meeting of the Canadian Federation of Biological Societies 14-17 June 1989 and 2nd Meeting of the International Society for Trace Element Research in Humans 8/89

11. Clarkson TW, Magos L, Greenwood MR: The transport of elemental mercury into fetal tissues. Biol Neonate 21:239-44, 1972

Chapter V
Discovering a Better Way to Chelate:
Why is the suppository method the better way?

Since its inception more than a half-century ago, chelation therapy has become widely accepted and practiced. From the well-studied standard intravenous (IV) method, which enjoys a high degree of clinical and published validation, chelation treatments have expanded to embrace variations of this proven modality. Recently, oral chelation supplements have become popular. And a revolutionary twist to the entire procedure has emerged with the advent of convenient chelation suppositories—now published and clinically validated as well.

In the past, I relied on IV chelation (a therapy where the EDTA is slowly introduced intravenously with a needle). I used this modality exclusively with my patients until I discovered the suppository method. Now, this is my mainstay therapy for thousands of them. Few people have the time, money and ability to tolerate the invasiveness of IV therapy. The suppository route is faster, more convenient, less expensive and proven effective. I still do IV therapies for those who request it, but the majority of my IV chelation treatments are done before and after the suppository regimens for accurate testing purposes. For those with extremely high loads of toxic metals, an initial round of intravenous chelation treatments simultaneously with suppository chelation is recommended. In this chapter, I examine the positive and negative aspects to these three approaches to chelation therapy.

IV chelation – It is true that, since its implementation as a medical procedure, IV EDTA chelation therapy has saved the lives and regained the health of people around the world. This therapy has given many people a second chance to pursue life, liberty and happiness. Intravenous chelation therapy works by pulling out heavy metals from difficult-to-reach areas within blood vessels, kidneys, and more. It may also reduce calcifications from arteries. Although it has been a boon and lifesaver, it also has disadvantages:

- *Not all physicians are trained in chelation therapy.* Therefore, a patient sometimes must travel several hours/miles to visit one.

1. *IV chelation is not convenient.* Once you arrive at the clinic, chelation is usually administered in 3000mg dosages in a procedure that lasts three to four hours. This is generally done once or twice a week, for 30 weeks or more.

2. *You can chelate too quickly and overtax the kidneys.* By forcing a chelation dose of 3 grams into the body over a short period of time, unnecessary stress is placed on organs of elimination, such as the kidneys. This is the rarest, but most cited, caution for IV chelation therapy. You can recover from the insult with smaller doses, spaced further apart.

3. *IV chelation isn't cheap.* It usually costs more than $150 per session, not even factoring in travel time and hours missed away from work. Do the math and you'll find this amount can add up to more than $4,500 a year! Due to

ongoing exposures to heavy metals, a maintenance session each month thereafter (for life) is recommended. Considering the toxic world in which we live, we all need maintenance solutions but IV chelation is an expensive way to go. However, I still give IV chelation to my patients who request it.

4. *Ideally, glass bottles should be used for IV treatments.* There are some studies that suggest plasticizers from the IV bags and tubing accumulate in the bloodstream and later end up contaminating the rest of the body. These plastics from IVs can quietly damage the chemistry needed by all cell membranes and thereby lead to further diseases, including high blood pressure. However, glass bottles greatly hike the cost of IV treatments and at that point you have to measure the risk of plastic bags versus the reward. I counter the toxicity of the plastic by giving my patients a high-dose antioxidant solution before beginning IV therapy, as well as between sessions.

Oral chelation –This method involves taking nutritional food supplements that contain chelating agents. Ingredients may include EDTA, as well as natural chelators like vitamins, minerals, amino acids, antioxidants, and herbs. Newer forms of volcanic ash derivative products are emerging and may prove useful to augment maintenance therapies. However, although convenient, oral chelation has its drawbacks, including:

- Only a small fraction of an oral EDTA dose is absorbed (compared with 100 percent of an IV dose).

- It takes much longer (if at all) for oral chelation to achieve anywhere similar results to that attained in just a few IV treatments. Oral chelation has never been shown to hold a candle to IV therapy. I tell people it's not worthless, but you'd better start oral chelation by age 15 to have any impact by age 50.
- Scientists and other members of the medical community aren't in complete agreement about the effectiveness of oral chelation, even among those who advocate chelation.

Chelation suppositories—This is an effective alternative to traditional IV EDTA chelation. The very same ingredient that goes into the IV (calcium disodium EDTA) has been incorporated into the rectal suppositories. This chelation delivery method is preferred by both myself *and* my patients because it can be done in the convenience of their own home and works safely and gently overnight.

New Forefront of Detoxification: Detoxamin
My heart aches that the world is heavy metal toxic, and that means each one of us. However, not everyone can afford IV chelation treatments. Therefore, I believe that Detoxamin chelation suppositories provide the answer to halting the oxidative damage we all experience from heavy metals. Each suppository has been proven in preclinical pharmacokinetic studies to deliver approximately 36 percent of what an IV dose offers. Compared to other rectal medicines, this delivery level is truly impressive. This route is the most medically similar to the traditional IV EDTA chelation method, but does not present the problems associated

with IV EDTA delivery. The dosage of EDTA is smaller; therefore, it does not put so much strain on the body, especially the kidneys. It is recommended that you use Detoxamin three to four times per week. Remember, research shows that Detoxamin stays in the blood stream around eight hours. If a higher dose is desired, under the care of a physician, patients might want to use the suppositories more frequently or use a prescription-dose level.

Each suppository contains 750mg of calcium disodium EDTA (about a quarter of regular IV dosage), which is slowly absorbed through the sigmoid colon (while you sleep) and gently works to remove heavy metals from the body. Nighttime detoxification is the most efficient, since that's when the oxidative stress load on the body is at its minimum, and the immune system's healing mechanisms are working at maximum. The body repairs cells and releases growth hormones around 10 p.m. so it's logical to conclude that the body ability to receive Detoxamin's antioxidant benefits would be ideal during this period. It is my belief that the antioxidant rescue of the 20th century was vitamin C. Detoxamin could be the antioxidant of the 21st century against the new enemy—heavy metal toxicity.

Of course, there is always an option to use IV chelation and the suppositories as combination treatment. Some of my patients are very sick and find they get a quicker and greater response when using the two types of chelation together. I know EDTA science is valid and, in my published study, proven tissue levels of EDTA provided by Detoxamin exceeded those of IV levels, and blood levels showed a more gentle level over eight hours in a biphasic manner for availability.

I trust Detoxamin because it is the most effective chelation system available today and is used by many physicians, healthcare professionals and consumers around the world. I believe Detoxamin is the leader in chelation suppositories because it has been carefully developed and researched by my staff and others. Detoxamin is backed by two clinical studies that have clearly proven scientifically its safety and medical similarity to IV EDTA chelation. I have also clinically proven its ability to remove heavy metal toxins in more than one thousand of my patients at the Tustin Longevity Center in Orange County and more than one million doses have been administered world wide.

I have seen clear evidence of this amazing product's efficacy and safety. It utilizes the power of calcium-disodium EDTA, the form of EDTA having the longest track record benefiting a wide variety of cardiovascular conditions, including hypertension, angina, claudication, congestive heart failure, and arrhythmias. It has also helped remove plaques blocking neck, heart and leg vessels, even in situations where surgery was contraindicated. EDTA is so safe, it has been FDA approved for more than six decades.

Questions and concerns

The suppositories are small and soft and are easy to use. However, I need to encourage some of my patients because they aren't familiar with using that particular route of delivery. I assure them that the long-term benefits outweigh any initial inconvenience.

Once a person gets past the initial psychological roadblock of rectal suppositories, subsequent administrations are very easy.

Detoxamin has undergone rigorous preclinical and clinical studies. I recommend it to my professional colleagues, whose skepticism resolves when they hear the facts, such as:

- The safety and efficacy of EDTA is unquestionable, backed by more than six decades of support by the FDA.
- Detoxamin has an impressive track record of proven success since the formula was developed in 1998.
- Scientific studies provide the hard evidence of Detoxamin's absorption, bio-availability and high tissue level concentration. No other brand of suppository can make this claim. If they do, tell them to show you the science they have conducted.
- All formulations offered by World Health Products have been reviewed and approved by a distinguished medical panel for safety and reliability.

When health professionals want to know the pathway in which the EDTA in Detoxamin works as compared to IV chelation, I can also answer that question, too. Detoxamin chelation suppositories are taken at night, right before a person retires for the evening. This allows less metabolic competition for the EDTA because the body is at rest while the EDTA works. The suppositories introduce less EDTA than IV chelation, but they are administered frequently, providing better EDTA assimilation. (This can be compared to taking vitamins, where a person takes less but more often).

Almost all of the blood from the rectum makes its way to the superior hemorrhoidal veins, a tributary of the portal system. The lower and middle hemorrhoidal veins bypass the liver and do not undergo first pass metabolism. Therefore, the EDTA in the suppositories are not filtered through the liver first, making the EDTA more productive by introducing EDTA directly into the circulatory and lymphatic systems.

Additionally, Detoxamin chelation suppositories are far safer than IV chelation because the EDTA in the suppositories travels through the body at a much slower rate, which alleviates an undue elimination burden on the liver and kidneys.

Another question that comes up frequently is whether a person should take replacement minerals when using the suppositories. I tell them it's a wise precaution to take, although I've never seen a mineral deficiency result from IV *or* suppository chelation therapies. I've conducted RBC mineral tests on my patients before and after chelation and I have not observed any significant changes. If any trend is noted, it is toward improved nutrient mineral status.

Advantages and benefits of suppositories vs. IV chelation
You save time. You chelate heavy metals from your system in the convenience of your home overnight. There are no worries about traveling long distances to sit for hours at a time, hooked up to an IV setup.

<u>Suppository chelation is safe</u>. Heavy metals are gently coaxed from the body with a quarter of the dose usually given by the IV method. (This relieves the kidneys and the rest of the body from the strain of forcing a higher dose on it over a shorter period of time).

<u>It is inexpensive</u>. A month's worth of the suppositories, used nightly for 30 days, costs roughly the equivalent of what you would pay for a single IV chelation session.

<u>You control the dosage</u>. You can easily adjust your timing and chelation schedule. For instance, you can chelate for one month and then rest or go 90 days and then take a break—it's up to you!

<u>More efficient, less invasive, 70% less expensive and safer</u>. By utilizing suppository delivery, the body will be able to process the product without having to filter it through protective channels in the liver and is therefore an efficient means for administering EDTA throughout the body.

Pharmaceutical-grade standards
World Health Products is the producer of Detoxamin. Their facility is registered with the United States Food and Drug Administration and manufactures the suppositories under the supervision of expert Ph.D.s in chemistry and nutrition. Additionally, their processes strictly follow Good Manufacturing Practices (GMPs). All ingredients are of the highest USP grade, with assays certifying potency and purity. World Health Products' state-of-the-art scientific quality-control testing laboratory ensures that you receive the highest quality products available.

Detoxamin is reasonably priced, considering the substantial health benefits it provides and is more affordable to those who have difficulty with the higher priced IV route of administration.

Detoxamin's Benefits

- Easy to administer
- Well tolerated by children and adults
- Enhances feelings of vitality, increased energy and well being
- Supports cardiovascular and bone health
- Clears toxic metal buildup in tissues
- Facilitates toxin elimination
- Provides continual slow-acting gentle detoxification during sleep
- Decreases free radical damage while protecting cells, tissues and organs from metal poisoning
- Supports healthy brain and neurological function while helping to maintain healthy body metabolism
- Diminishes the accelerated aging process
- Offers gentle, noninvasive and safe slow absorption
- Compatible and complementary with IV chelation

Comparison of IV Chelation and CaNa$_2$ EDTA Suppositories (Detoxamin)

	IV Chelation	Rectal Suppositories
Non-Invasive	No	Yes
Quick and easy to use	No	Yes
Inexpensive	No	Yes
Increased safety	No	Yes
Broad spectrum metal removal	Yes	Yes
FDA approved	Yes	Yes
Clinically proven	Yes	Yes

Additional advantages over IV EDTA chelation

The following information is based on proprietary IV EDTA comparison studies:

- Detoxamin maintains over an 8-hour half-life, compared to 1.5 hours half-life for a single IV EDTA treatment. A significant finding: long-lasting EDTA blood levels offer more time to efficiently chelate for slow, gentle, effective and safe chelation.
- Detoxamin is 36.3 percent bioequivalent to IV chelation— medically similar to proven IV EDTA chelation.
- Significant, efficient long-lasting EDTA blood levels enable more efficient heavy metal clearance.
- Detoxamin saturates the tissues three-fold more deeply than does IV EDTA chelation, and has been established through pre-clinical studies. This is significant since Detoxamin can reach and remove heavy metals right where they are located. Improved tissue saturation of EDTA gives greater protection to cells, tissues and organs.

Pharmacokinetic Results of IV vs Rectal Suppository Administration

	Intravenous	Rectal (Suppositories)*
Absolute Bioavailability	100%	36.3 %
Blood to Tissue Ratio**	3.7	13.6
Half-Life	1.5 hours	8 hours +

* Detoxamin
** Prostate tissue

In one study conducted under my supervision at Tustin Longevity Center, 31 men (average age 61) with chronic prostatitis and benign prostate hyperplasia (BPH) showed the benefits of this improved tissue saturation. Participants were treated with 500 mg/day of tetracycline and Detoxamin suppositories four times a week for 90 days. Using the NIH Chronic Prostatitis Symptom Index, significant post-treatment reductions in prostatitis symptoms and pain were found, along with a significant improvement in quality of life. Analysis of blood and stool post-treatment indicated significant excretions of heavy metals such as lead, cadmium, arsenic, tungsten, copper, and molybdenum. This research suggests that a combination therapy of tetracycline and Detoxamin may be a viable means to reduce signs and symptoms of prostatitis/pelvic pain and benign prostate hyperplasia.

In another study, men with BPH used the 1500 mg Detoxamin suppository nightly for 90 days, along with 500 mg of tetracycline and a multi-mineral and probiotic supplement. The patients showed even more significant statistically improved cardiovascular parameters and most amazingly, their prostate calcifications were noted by radiology to start dissolving. Calcium always shows up whenever there is tissue injury or chronic inflammation, including that from oxidative stress and free radical damage from heavy metals. This mineral helps with coagulation, responding as a healing emergency medical technician where there is injury. Once the cells and tissues are okay, then the calcium dissipates.

So the presence of calcium in the body is a prime indicator of an area calling for attention. However, with ongoing trauma and stress in the body, calcium is constantly part of the damage repair team. Eventually, calcifications (a build-up of insoluble calcium salts) can initiate many disease processes and impair proper blood circulation.

In all Detoxamin studies I've researched and published on thus far, only benefits have accrued. The safety and efficacy have been established with standard laboratory and diagnostic methodologies. More Detoxamin studies are forthcoming and I'm honored to have been selected as one of the principal investigators. Positive results in my patients are encouraging, but clinical research validates them in a scientific way. Read in the next chapter about my total approach to wellness. I use Detoxamin as the key to removing oxidative heavy metal toxins and then take the therapy a step further. I add key nutritional supplements with lipid replacement therapy to help repair oxidative damage from other environmental contaminants and revitalize the cell membrane.

Chapter VI
Cutting Edge Combo Therapy

Every day your body has to deal with toxic metal pollutants. From cookware, canned goods, soda pop cans and cosmetics to medications and even mineral supplements containing excess iron, you are saturated daily in a bath of metal toxins. (And remember those herbs from overseas with lead in them!). They generate free radicals that cause oxidative damage. You and your cells are at risk from silent accumulations of this oxidative damage over the years—leading to chronic and debilitating diseases.

Look in your kitchen cupboards, your refrigerator, your medicine cabinet, your cosmetic bag, your personal care products shelf. How many times do you grab a soda when you're thirsty? (I never recommend using them).Want to know what's going on with the weather? Go outside and look up at the sky. Chances are, besides fluffy clouds and sunshine, you'll see air pollution wafting in from factory emissions and trails of jet fuel exhaust. Remember, nearly 5,000 airplanes fly over us every day.

What's that whiff of smoke coming around the corner from your house? Could it be your neighbor puffing out cadmium ions while smoking on the porch of the house next door? The above scenarios describe just a fraction of the ways your body is exposed daily to these toxic metals.

The most common toxic metals are mercury, lead, aluminum, cadmium and arsenic. They stimulate the production of free radicals that collect in the human system and damage the cardiovascular and nervous systems, as well as tissues, bones and vital organs such as the liver and kidneys. The result? A plethora of diseases more prevalent today than ever before in recorded history. Since the industrial revolution, the use of heavy metals to create products and packaged energy such as batteries and petrochemical fuels has skyrocketed. And remember that these toxic metals have been linked to a wide range of health issues— from learning disorders to cancer and heart disease.

It has been estimated that the average bone lead level of a person today is 1,000 times greater than of a person living 400 years ago. And researchers report that ailing hearts have 20,000 times more toxic metals than healthy ones.

I have found in my practice that many (if not all) diseases can be reduced and often reversed using what I call the "remove, repair, and revitalize" approach. Since everyone is contaminated with heavy metals that damage cell membranes and reduce blood flow, promoting disease and aging, I put all my patients on Detoxamin. Then I complement this approach with therapeutic lifestyle changes, followed by research-proven and published products that help repair the cell membranes and put them in a positive direction to abundant health. Following is a description of my simple yet very effective program, starting with Detoxamin. (I've talked a bit about Detoxamin earlier in this book. But it is such an amazing product that I want to review it again with you).

Detoxamin is a rectal suppository that contains the chelating ingredient calcium disodium EDTA. This substance binds and removes or decreases toxic oxidative metal levels in your body. My patients find that the bullet-shaped suppositories are easy to insert and they don't even feel them once they are in place. The body's normal temperature naturally dissolves the cocoa butter, which allows the EDTA to spread over the lower intestinal tract lining. Over an hour and a half period, it is absorbed directly into the bloodstream. It is interesting to note that the half-life of EDTA IV chelation is 1.5 hours, while Detoxamin's suppository has a half-life of more than eight hours. This makes Detoxamin gentle, safe, and effective over a longer period of time as compared to IV chelation.

Because Detoxamin chelation suppositories are taken at night, they do not interfere with my patients' daytime schedule. This also works better from a physiological standpoint because at night there are far less internal metabolic activities to compete with the EDTA chelating process. This innovative suppository method introduces less dosage of EDTA when compared to the IV chelation method, but the more frequent administration allows for a much higher chelation efficiency.

I know that Detoxamin is also superior to oral chelation products because EDTA is readily absorbed by the colon. The technical pathway works like this: because the rectum has a more neutral pH and is not as acidic as the stomach, the EDTA passes through intact—allowing for very high EDTA absorption. This is what I mean by "bioavailability," which we've referred to before. It is interesting to note that only about seven percent of the EDTA in oral chelation products is absorbed by the body.

Although the EDTA from the suppositories moves much slower than IV EDTA, it remains longer throughout the body and does not burden the liver or kidneys. This feature allows the EDTA more time to chelate, as well as makes it safer for the body. It isn't filtered by the liver and so is immediately received into the bloodstream.

As a physician, I am impressed that Detoxamin's efficacy is validated through clinical trials and numerous studies that prove calcium disodium EDTA removes a broad spectrum of heavy metals from human tissues. This is a supreme chelating substance because it has the most comprehensive ability to remove all varieties of heavy metals.

How to Use Detoxamin:

If you are using Detoxamin under the care of a health care professional, please follow their advice. However, the general recommendations for use of Detoxamin are as follows:

Take one Detoxamin suppository every other night prior to bedtime. Take a good multi vitamin and mineral daily. Drink plenty of water and stay well hydrated. If you have never detoxified with chelation therapy in the past, it is recommended to use Detoxamin as described above for at least six months. This will require 90 suppositories or three of the Detoxamin 30-count containers. After this initial program, it is recommended to continue using one suppository every week thereafter as on-going maintenance for detoxification of heavy metals.

DOSAGE LEVEL FOR DETOXAMIN
Detoxamin comes in three dosage levels for consumers to choose from; **375mg** for people or children under 100lbs, **750mg** for people between 100lbs.-175lbs., and **1000mg** for people over 175lbs.

Vital Cellular Nutrition with NT Factor: **REPAIR & REVITALIZE**
While Detoxamin removes the heavy metals and toxins from the bloodstream, *Vital Cellular Nutrition with NT Factor* helps repair **and** nourish the cell membrane so it can function at its optimal best. This process is vital for cellular health and the health of your entire body.

The nutrients contained in *Vital Cellular Nutrition with NT Factor* have been carefully selected and blended for maximum benefit. Their beneficial properties are recognized by the scientific community and are validated by studies published in peer-reviewed medical journals. There is a chance that chelation may remove some essential elements, although I have never seen this as a problem in my patients. Therefore, *Vital Cellular Nutrition with NT Factor* has been fortified with key minerals—and it's a good idea, anyway, to supplement them in the diet.

Vital Cellular Nutrition with NT Factor facilitates efficient nutrient uptake by the cell membrane. The innovative technology to accomplish this task is called "lipid replacement therapy" (LRT). This action enables fresh phospholipids to replace the "broken lipids" throughout the cell membranes of your body. By replenishing the fatty components that make up this structure, it restores cell membrane stability and thus helps the body experience vitality and energy once again.

In one clinical trial, the ability to produce cellular energy was improved to the point that subjects whose average age was 70 years old experienced the level of energy corresponding to that of healthy 30-year-olds! Researchers validated the increased energy reported by participants through blood cell extractions. Extent of energy improvement and relief from fatigue reported via surveys paralleled the laboratory data.

Vital Cellular Nutrition with NT Factor contains a comprehensive variety of beneficial nutrients, packed in one supplement. Containing four tablets and one soft gel capsule in convenient packets, this product supplies EFA-rich fish oils and an impressive range of beneficial moderately dosed vitamins, minerals, probiotics and antioxidants. I want to emphatically stress that you need less of each nutrient when the cellular membranes and internal organ membranes work efficiently with the previously explained improved circulation. This helps the cell to utilize these nutrients and further enhances absorption of nutrients from food. That translates into dollars saved on research-established nutraceuticals and protocols, making your money work for you!

Peer-reviewed published clinical studies show that *Vital Cellular Nutrition with NT Factor:*

- Restored mitochondrial function in the elderly to levels normal for young healthy adults in eight weeks.
- Eliminated severe fatigue in eight weeks.
- Restored optimal nutrient absorption in 8 weeks (via membrane potential, the controller for all cell transport).
- Reduced adverse effects of chemotherapy such as fatigue and other chemotherapy-induced toxicities.

In animal studies, *Vital Cellular Nutrition with NT Factor:*

- Virtually stopped the age-related loss of energy and nerve function in animals fed the formula.
- Stopped age-related accumulation of genetic damage.

As mentioned earlier, your vitality is powered by dozens to thousands of mitochondria—minute structures scattered throughout every cell in your body. Mitochondria are combustion chambers that transform nutrients and oxygen into usable energy. In order for the mitochondria to work properly inside the cell, nutrients must be absorbed first through the outer cell membrane. However, if that membrane is damaged, the membrane surrounding the mitochondria is vulnerable to attack by free radicals and the body's energy production greatly diminishes. This leads to a myriad of health disorders, including the very prevalent complaint of today: fatigue.

Vital Cellular Nutrition with NT Factor acts as "mitochondrial fuel" and is a core product specifically developed to mend damaged cell membranes. It contains NT Factor--the ingredient blend designed to heal the oxidative damage and cell membrane "holes" caused by free radicals. This product features a unique extract of polyunsaturated, fractionated phospholipids—natural lipids or fats—that help replenish the cell membrane. This formula actually supplies nutrition that the cell recognizes and that it can utilize to repair itself. When the mitochondria function at an optimal level, my patients experience youthful vibrancy, increased energy levels and improved quality of life.

The special fatty acid complex has flexibility to permeate both fat and water components of the cell membrane, ensuring a thorough repair job. The unique characteristics of *Vital Cellular Nutrition with NT Factor* allow cells the freedom to grow, replicate and absorb nutrients for energy. Some of my patients like to take *Energy Factor*, (NT Factor only), as a complement to their favorite multi-vitamin supplement.

From a scientific point of view, it is interesting to note that the phospholipids in *Vital Cellular Nutrition with NT Factor* help the cell connect with the world around it. It helps signal to hormones and other substances, thus keeping the body's communication pathways in top shape. Phospholipids also nourish the brain and nerve membranes. This beneficial action helps keep the central nervous system running smoothly.

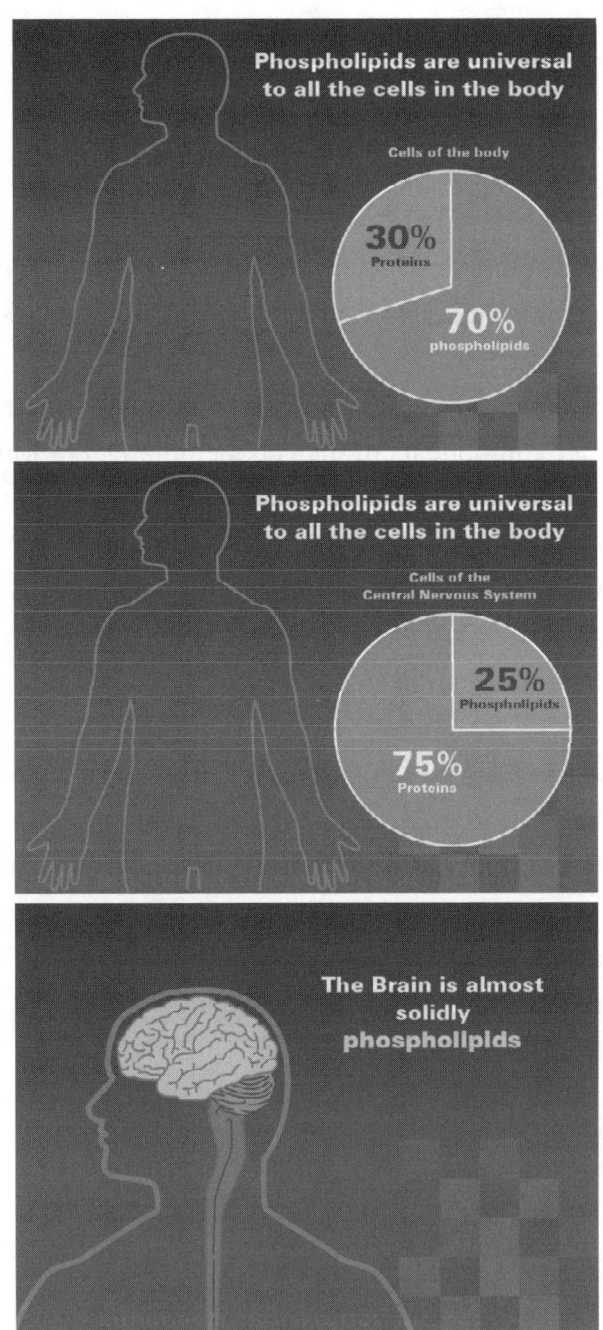

In my practice, I have found that many symptoms of neuro-degenerative diseases like Alzheimer's, Parkinson's disease, and multiple sclerosis—as well as fatiguing illnesses and the insulin resistance disorder called metabolic syndrome–respond favorably to the remove, repair and revitalize program. Once you remove toxic metals, then restore proper membrane function, the cells can once again send signals, correcting gaps in the information exchange.

You can't work under a leaky roof
I dispense products tailored to specific conditions, all enhanced with the inclusion of NT Factor. This is the key to ensuring membrane health. One of my favorite analogies I tell my patients is this: imagine you are sitting in an office trying to do your work, but the roof has holes in it and birds are flying in and out. The wind is blowing and your papers are flying all around. It's chaos. You might be the most professional person and the one best suited to your job, but if your "shell" is broken, you can't perform your duties. This is the same way for a cell. Membrane health and "wholeness" is just as important as the nutrient trying to nourish it. The nutrient can't be effective when it just leaks out of the cell because of a broken membrane.

In the next chapter, I'll describe impressive health improvements experienced by some of my patients who went on the "remove, repair and revitalize" program.

References

1. "China exports lead poisoning: From eye shadow to glazed pottery, products pose danger to U.S. kids." Posted June 7, 2007. (www.worldnetdaily.com; accessed 6/23/08).
2. Agadjanyan M, Vasilevko V, Ghochikyan A, Berns P, Kesslak P, Settineri R, Nicolson G. Nutritional Supplement (NT Factor™) Restores Mitochondrial Function and Reduces Moderately Severe Fatigue in Aged Subjects." Clinical Publications and Scientific Validation for Propax with NT Factor® and NT Factor®: Advances in Lipid Replacement Technology for Cellular Energy Improvement and Cellular Membrane Repair.
3. Ellithorpe, RR, Settineri RA, Nicolson GL. Pilot Study: Reduction of Fatigue by Use of a Dietary Supplement Containing Glycophospholipids. Clinical Publications and Scientific Validation for Propax with NT Factor® and NT Factor®: Advances in Lipid Replacement Technology for Cellular Energy Improvement and Cellular Membrane Repair.
4. Ibid.
5. Ibid.
6. Colodny L, Lynch K, Farber C, Papish S, Phillips K, et al. Results of a Study to Evaluate the Use of Propax™ to Reduce Adverse Effects of Chemotherapy. Clinical Publications and Scientific Validation for Propax with NT Factor® and NT Factor®: Advances in Lipid Replacement Technology for Cellular Energy Improvement and Cellular Membrane Repair.

Chapter VII
Actual Case Studies

I've studied the presence of heavy metals in over 3,000 patients using Doctor's Data (St. Charles, IL) to perform the metal analyses. Packed red blood cell analyses of one hundred percent of these patients show the presence of heavy metals above acceptable levels. When these patients use the Detoxamin chelation suppositories, their circulation is enhanced and there is a notable improvement in general well being.

Other benefits include increased energy and endurance and better mental clarity from enhanced nutrient delivery and detoxification. These patients also experience reduced blood pressure levels and improved erectile function. Laboratory studies also show reductions in inflammation and HDL cholesterol improvements are noted.

As a physician, it is rewarding to see my patients make progress from seemingly insurmountable obstacles with their health. Following are just a few examples from the thousands of patients I have treated successfully over the years.

Patient #1

K.M. was in her early fifties when she first sought treatment. She had gone on disability from teaching due to severe low back pain, chronic fatigue, postmenopausal symptoms and hypothyroidism. She was on several prescription medications. She was seeking natural therapies and detoxification to improve her energy and menopausal symptoms. During her evaluation for oxidative stress, red blood cell analysis indicated the excess presence of four heavy metals: lead, arsenic, mercury and cadmium. Along with a standard intravenous (I.V.) chelation treatment of 1.5 grams $CaNa_2EDTA$, I gave her a "heavy metal challenge" using oral DMSA (a substance used to provoke heavy metals from tissue). This protocol was used in conjunction with a six-hour urine collection for heavy metal analysis. She received 750 mg of rectal CaNa2EDTA (Detoxamin) suppositories three nights a week (total of 90 suppositories) and completed this regimen within 7 ½ months. After 9 ½ months, she returned for a repeat I.V. challenge identical to the first treatment. Even when using suppositories just twice a week, she had a large drop in mercury and lead levels in her blood cells. Although $CaNa_2EDTA$ is primarily an approved chelator for lead, I have seen multiple toxic heavy metals chelated by Detoxamin, which has a very good safety record.

K.M. remained on a maintenance dose of one suppository a week on the average for one year. When tested at that time, she continued to maintain reduced levels of heavy metals, despite consuming fish with probable mercury exposure. With exercise three times a week, she also experienced lessened back pain and improved energy. This patient is typical of those who continue to use Detoxamin suppositories for over six months on at least an average of twice a week.

Practical Clinical Case Study

Patient K.M.

55 y/o • W • F • 131 lbs. • School Teacher • Chronic LBP • Fatigue • Hypothyroid

Date	Cadium	Mercury	Lead	Nickel
5/03	1.7	30	43	9.5
2/04	1.0	2.6	27	17
2/05	1.0	18	27	13

Outcome: 7/04 – Excellent energy • Exercise 3x/day – water aerobics • Back pain stable • Reduced need for medications.

Patient #2

F.K. is a 42 year-old perimenopausal woman who worked in photography and developed chronic fatigue, hypothyroidism and insomnia. She also sought as natural as possible a means to improve her energy, sleep and oxidative stress. As expected, she also had above threshold levels of several toxic heavy metals, including arsenic, on a random red blood cell analysis. She was given the same heavy metal challenge with 500 mg oral DMSA and her urine was collected six hours later. At six hours her arsenic levels were elevated, along with significant elevations in cadmium, lead, mercury, and nickel. She then received Detoxamin rectal suppositories (750 mg), three nights a week.

Patient #2 was very compliant and kept up with the three nights per week treatments, and the challenge was repeated, as above, five months later. We normally treat for at least six months or a minimum of 60 suppositories, which most patients usually accomplish by the sixth or seventh month. Patient #2 was motivated since she knew her photography work exposed her to heavy metals and other toxins and she was concerned about the elevated arsenic levels. Interestingly, arsenic is found in chicken meat which she primarily consumed as her main source of protein.

According to *Chemical & Engineering News*, an arsenic-based additive used in chicken feed is linked to multiple health risks in humans.

By the fourth month, the arsenic level in F.K. dropped dramatically, as well as her other toxic metals (Figure 5). She continued on a maintenance dose of one 750 mg suppository weekly. Her 10-month challenge showed fairly good maintenance of the reductions in heavy metals. On follow up, K.M. admitted she skipped some doses and continued to enjoy chicken, although she used free-range chicken more often. She reported improved energy and was able to exercise daily for 45 minutes. She reduced her need for pain medications, had improved sleep and reduced perimenopausal symptoms.

Practical Clinical Case Study

Patient F.K.

42 y/o • W • F • 145 lbs. • Photographer • Fibromyalgia • Chronic Fatigue • Hypothyroid

Date	Arsenic	Cadium	Lead	Mercury	Nickel
8/02	220	2.5	20	24	49
12/02	4.5	2.1	7.4	15	25
5/03	45	3.2	12	8.9	18

Outcome: 11/04 – Energy good • Exercises daily (45 min.) with mild to moderate pain of fibromyalgia • Increased daily activities

Patient #3

M.O. is a 52-year-old male who worked as an electrician. He was experiencing palpitations and anxiety and began to visit emergency rooms more often as his symptoms worsened, despite normal cardiovascular examinations. He was placed on antidepressant and anti-anxiety medication. He was also given a medication to reduce palpitations.

Because of the high association of heavy metals with cardiac and neurological disease, we also did a random red blood cell analysis and found above accepted levels of four heavy metals. The same I.V. challenge was administered. He expressed an aversion to using rectal suppositories but used them at least half of the time. Instead of the recommended three nights a week he used one or two on the average, at most. Nevertheless, he showed reductions in heavy metals upon his repeat challenge five months later. The challenge was repeated four months later as he wanted reassurance that this was, in fact, reducing these toxins, despite not using the recommended dose per week. He found that his anxiety and palpitations were notably reduced and did not have any more emergency room visits.

M.O. continued using the suppositories once a week or less for eight months and another challenge was performed. Mercury showed an increased level above his initial reading. However, he had his amalgams partially removed, which we felt caused some mercury contamination, in addition to his exposure in food and possibly work materials. Subsequently, his motivation to use the suppositories increased, and he used them at least twice a week. Seven months later, we found reductions again in heavy metals in his
blood. We noted that his nickel levels varied, and we concluded that his exposure to nickel in his occupation also varied. With major reductions in lead and mercury, this may have allowed for the $CaNa_2EDTA$ to remove more nickel with continued use of the suppositories.

Practical Clinical Case Study

Patient M.O.

52 y/o • M • 175 lbs. • Electrician • Chronic Anxiety Panic Attacks • Hypertension • LBP

Date	Cadium	Mercury	Lead	Nickel
10/02	1.2	5.2	27	8.4
2/03	0.9	4.4	18	3.6
10/03	1.4	9.8	20	1.6
5/04	0.7	3.8	16	7.7
12/04	1.0	1.6	12	12

Outcome: 10/04 – Anxiety greatly improved • Reduced need for auxiolytic medication • Improved BP • Reduced anti-hypertensive medication • LBP improved • Exercises daily (30 min.)

This is only a small sampling showing individual case histories, but I continually find similar results with the majority of my patients.

Chapter VIII
The Bright Future of Chelation Therapy

Never before in the world's recorded history have humans experienced the onslaught of chronic disease as in our modern day. It definitely reflects the increasing toxicity we have experienced since the advent of the Industrial Age more than a century ago.

Based on my clinical research and observations of my patients, I know that toxic metals and other pollutants are the most significant, (yet overlooked or out rightly ignored) principal causes of today's rampant diseases.

In fact, deaths resulting from heavy metal oxidative damage have increased to the point that the government has had to adjust—even lower—previously accepted thresholds of toxicity. Scientists at institutions like the Centers for Disease Control have found that even low levels of those (such as lead) build up in the cells and tissues, damaging them slowly over time until symptoms of chronic heart disease or cancer appear.

Did you know that cancer is one of the top causes of death in children ages one through fourteen? And who is doing anything about this shocking fact? Today's exposure to pollutants is constantly making news and now we are learning that babies are poisoned before they are even born! Consider this headline from a report dated May 25, 2007 in the *Los Angeles Times* article "Common chemicals pose danger for fetuses, scientists warn: Exposure to toxic materials in the womb can cause health problems later in life, an international panel declares." Following is an excerpt from this article:

"In a strongly worded declaration, many of the world's leading environmental scientists warned Thursday that exposure to common chemicals makes babies more likely to develop an array of health problems later in life, including diabetes, attention deficit disorders, prostate cancer, fertility problems, thyroid disorders and even obesity.

"The declaration by about 200 scientists from five continents amounts to a vote of confidence in a growing body of evidence that humans are vulnerable to long-term harm from toxic exposures in the womb and during their first years.

" 'Given the ubiquitous exposure to many environmental toxicants, there needs to be renewed efforts to prevent harm. Such prevention should not await detailed evidence on individual hazards,' the scientists wrote in the four-page statement."

Turn the tide

The reason I went into the field of medicine is so I could help those who are ill and suffering. My heart really goes out to people who are looking for answers, but do not know where to turn. My motto is "to conquer the enemy, you have to understand him." That's so true in the area of disease. As I've emphasized before, first you identify the culprits causing the problems. Second, you remove them so they can't do any more harm. Third, you repair the damage already done and last, you give the body the nutrition it needs for maximum health. This combination approach is what my "remove, repair, revitalize" program is all about. Following is a synopsized recap of my three-step program for abundant health.

The problem: toxins

Every day your body has to deal with metal toxins from a range of sources, inside the home and out. These contaminants generate free radicals, which cause oxidative damage to your cells. Your entire body is then at risk from silent accumulations of this oxidative damage over the years—leading to chronic and debilitating disease.

The solution: remove, repair, revitalize

Remove harmful heavy metal accumulations with Detoxamin chelation suppositories. Detoxamin is gentle, safe and effective over a longer period of time than IV chelation. Detoxamin suppositories are also very convenient. Because they are taken at night, they do not interfere with daytime routines. Detoxamin is superior to IV chelation because now the world can protect itself affordably against environmental toxins. Intravenous chelation is not an option for most people because they can't afford it, don't have the time for the initial 30 IV treatments and they can't keep up the monthly IVs for the duration of their lifetime. And the best news is, calcium disodium EDTA is the primo ingredient recognized for its ability to remove a broad spectrum of heavy metals from human tissues. This powerful and supreme chelating substance has the most comprehensive ability to remove all varieties of heavy metals. Detoxamin should be used on an ongoing basis because exposure to toxic metals never stops. However, Detoxamin can be used along with IV chelation.

Suppositories and IV, in combination, will pull you out of the problems caused by heavy metal exposure. I go where the data is, and science undergirds these approaches. Only use products that have been scientifically validated. You don't get a copycat life, so don't use copycat products. Your health is too important.

I never recommend oral chelation because it is not aggressive enough and the stakes (your life and health) are too high. Because cancer and heart disease are linked to heavy metal toxicity, you want to use treatments that work. Don't be fooled by impostor products.

Remember, outer membranes are the first line of defense for your cells, your body's foundation for tissues, organs and systems. And you must have the circulation cleared down to the level of your capillaries. These membranes protect against invaders that can breach the inner membranes lining the mitochondria, the intra-cellular chambers responsible for the birthplace of your energy.

Repair & Revitalize is the second and third step respectively and can be accomplished with *Vital Cellular Nutrition with NT Factor.* The formula contains the critical phospholipid ingredients that repair cell membrane damage.   There are two more products offered by World Health Products, the maker of Detoxamin, that contain this cellular repair quality if you already use a good multi-vitamin and mineral.

1. *RepairACell* contains NT factor for cellular repair, plus essential minerals.
2. *Energy Factor* contains just the NT factor for cellular repair alone. These choices are less expensive than the all-in-one

formula of *Vital Cellular Nutrition with NT Factor.* I love
this selection because it creates affordability for any type
of income.

My patients who wish to take advantage of the ultimate in cellular
nutritional research, along with Detoxamin suppositories, choose
the *Vital Cellular Nutrition with NT Factor* formula. *Vital Cellular
Nutrition with NT Factor* also contains a comprehensive
antioxidant profile, along with essential fatty acids, as well as the
phospholipids and probiotics of NT Factor—the critical
components of membrane repair and revitalization. It contains the
widest range of nutrition offered by the "remove, repair,
revitalize" program. Besides containing key nutritional factors, it
works with the heavy metal chelation suppositories to also
detoxify the body of environmental poisons such as PCBs,
plasticizers and other foreign chemicals prevalent in today's
world. I personally use *Vital Cellular Nutrition with NT Factor*
because I see so many sick and dying people in my occupation
and I want to use the highest nutritional fortification possible.

I want to mention that during the detoxification process it is
possible to feel worse when your body is "cleaning house." I tell
my patients in advance not to be alarmed if they experience
headaches or other aches and pains, sneezing—even nausea and
fatigue—when embarking on a detoxification regime. This can be
normal and the symptoms will gradually dissipate in days to
weeks. Sometimes you have to feel worse to feel better. I tell them
it's like organizing your closets. You throw everything out in a

heap and it's a mess at first, then you eliminate the unwanted items and put the good things back neatly on the shelf.

To minimize this effect, I suggest my patients hydrate with 64 to 80 ounces of water daily, avoid refined carbohydrates, and engage in aerobic exercise (like walking or stationary bicycling) for 30 minutes each day. I also encourage them to take systemic proteolytic enzymes, like bromelain, to help clean up cellular debris in the body.

Future research

I am so excited about the widespread potential of the Detoxamin combo program, I have become involved in ongoing research. As a team principal investigator of many studies, future plans include the following:

(1) *Firefighter study*—The people who protect our homes and other structures from fire damage are they, themselves, exposed to harm in the process. Because their respiratory systems are literally "under fire" from inhaling fumes of toxic burning materials, many people in this occupation come down with unexplainable symptoms. We want to put them on the three-part program and monitor their progress throughout the course of the study.

(2) *Autism study*—Several symptoms of autism parallel those of mercury poisoning and many scientists and health professionals believe that exposure to this toxic metal plays a crucial role in both the onset and progression of the disease. We anticipate doing a study on groups of children with diagnosed autism. We will put

them on a modified program with Detoxamin for Kids and evaluate their improvement over a significant period of time.

(3) *BPH study*—Since we've seen an impressive reduction of symptoms in our first prostate health study, we are developing another study to research the toxic metal connection to benign prostatic hyperplasia (BPH).

(4) *Microcalcifications study*—Excessive calcium deposits (microcalcifications) reflect chronic cell membrane damage. They have been linked to many disorders, including fibrocystic breast disease, kidney stones, osteoarthritis and peripheral artery disease. Power color doplar sonagraphy (PCD) can detect these microcalcifications because chronic cell membrane injury attracts the normal inflammatory response, which always involves calcium deposits. These calculi show up as white specks against the dark film. PCD is my detection method of choice and I employ this modality right in my office. Cell injury means inflammation—and inflammation is known as pain and felt as heat. Because we know that it enhances circulation to every part of the body and eliminates oxidative damage, we plan on investigating the possibility that the remove, repair and revitalize approach can reduce or reverse these symptoms. For updates on our ongoing research, please visit www.detoxamin.com.

Tips for Minimizing Exposure to Heavy Metal Toxins
1. Avoid deodorants with aluminum ingredients.
2. Avoid antacids with aluminum ingredients.
3. Avoid vaccines with the mercury preservative thimerosal.

4. Avoid brightly colored, cheap lead-paint jewelry.
5. Avoid drinking water from older homes with lead pipes.
6. Avoid using chemical fertilizers.
7. Remove "silver" amalgams from your teeth. (Undergo this procedure with a holistic-minded dentist familiar with the proper procedure).
8. Purify your water with a reverse osmosis (RO) filter.
9. Remove heavy metal ions from the air in your home with an air filter.
10. Avoid cigarette smoke.
11. Use unbleached (instead of bleached) flour.
12. Do not breathe automobile exhaust.
13. Avoid using commercial laxatives containing the mercury ingredient calomel.
14. Consume smaller fish. I tell my patients if it can fit easily in a frying pan or roaster, its okay to eat. Larger predatory fish like tuna or swordfish contain more heavy metals, like mercury. Size matters when choosing your fish!
15. Dispose of batteries properly.
16. Use protective precautions when soldering or welding.
17. Avoid using synthetic pesticides.
18. Before you purchase wood for construction purposes, check for the presence of wood preservatives, like arsenic.
19. Be careful of cosmetics (especially lipsticks, eye shadows and hair dyes). Many cosmetic products need to be screened and examined. However, this industry is not regulated by the FDA and many of them contain heavy metals (i.e., black hair dyes may contain lead).

My Other Recommendations for Improved Health

- Manage stress – don't take on more than you can handle
- Get enough sleep – 8 is the magic number
- Eat a balanced diet – plenty of unsprayed fruits, vegetables and whole grains
- Reduce carbohydrates
- Drink non-fluoridated, non-chlorinated water – half your weight in pounds as ounces
- Exercise on a regular basis – even if it's just walking for 30 minutes a day

Please note: Many medications and some pharmaceutical products contain heavy metals. By law, if it's under a threshold of volume, it doesn't have to be declared on the label and the inclusion in the listing is not mandatory. Such is the case with thimerosal, the mercury ingredient in vaccines. It's still there, just in smaller non-reportable quantities. (The FDA still allows amounts at sub-threshold levels but even small amounts of metals have a cumulative impact). When one is exposed to five, 10 and sometimes 20 of them a day, this chronic exposure becomes a significant factor. It doesn't make sense to me that we can warn pregnant women against consuming certain types of fish because of the mercury but we can't warn her against getting amalgam fillings put into her mouth. The American Dental Association discourages your dentist against associating any disease with mercury usage in his practice.

Do Not Be Deceived

There are companies who claim to have chelation suppository formulas similar to or even identical to that of Detoxamin. However, World Health Products was the first company that developed NaCa$_2$ EDTA chelation suppositories and is the only company that has invested hundreds of thousands of dollars in independent third-party research and studies. These other companies "piggyback" off of their efforts in order to claim the same level of efficacy. While imitation is said to be the highest form of compliment, in this case it does not serve the consumer's best interests. I know that World Health Products manufactures Detoxamin in a Good Manufacturing Practices (GMP) approved facility. If you are in doubt in making a decision of what product is best, ask other companies if they have research published in reputable peer-reviewed journals on their specific product formulas. If they cannot provide the studies then why use something that has not been proven?

I am impressed that Detoxamin's absorption, bio-availability, and high tissue concentrations are validated through scientific research. Each formula developed by World Health Products has been reviewed and approved by a distinguished medical panel for safety and reliability. In summary, I feel that Detoxamin is a superior product because it is of the highest quality and holds an enviable track record of success.

My entire family—myself, my husband, my two sons, and even our parents—chelate with Detoxamin on a regular basis. Through testing, I found out that my sons (now young adults) had elevated levels of mercury in their teens. I discovered it was from my amalgams I had when I was pregnant with them. So I was the biggest swordfish!

The amazing outlook for chelation therapy
Although I am a practicing physician, I compare today's American medical system to the old British military fighting methods. Their line of attack involved shooting at the enemy while they themselves were exposed to view in open fields. They were completely vulnerable to fire from enemy snipers in outlying hedges and trees. This reminds me of today's standard therapeutic policies. If we don't take a proactive stance in protecting our health and use the same archaic model of fixing things after they are broken, we will be shot and killed by toxins in our food, water, personal care products, etc. We need a new tactic.

That's why I believe that the Detoxamin combo therapy should be a big part of changing this approach. The power of chelation suppositories, augmented by cell membrane repair through improved circulation and nutritional supplementation, can create a new paradigm for health. Not just mediocre health, but vitality, vigor and energy—paving the way for life—the way it's meant to be lived!

(Please visit my Web site, www.tlcmd.net, for further information regarding medical presentations on detoxification and other valuable health-related topics).

References

1. University of Pennsylvania Health System. Death among children and adolescents. (www.pennhealth.com; accessed 6/26/07).
2. Ejaz ul Islam, Xiao-e Yang, Zhen-li He, Qaisar Mahmood. Assessing potential dietary toxicity of heavy metals in selected vegetables and food crops. J Zhejiang Univ. Sci. B. 2007 January; 8(1):1-13.

Additional Resources

1. www.tlcmd.net – Tustin Longevity Center. Dr. Ellithorpe's Clinic
2. www.detoxamin.com – World Health Product, LLC - Detoxamin chelation suppositories; heavy metal toxicity information
3. www.doctorsdata.com – Doctor's Data Inc. - Heavy metal toxicity testing
4. www.acam.org – American College for Advancement in Medicine - Information on chelation
5. www.worldhealth.net – American Academy of Anti-Aging Medicine – Nutrition and natural supplement information
6. www.aaemonline.org – American Academy of Environmental Medicine – Information on optimal health through prevention and safe and effective treatment
7. "Questions and Answers: The NIH Trial of EDTA Chelation Therapy for Coronary Artery Disease". National Center for Complementary and Alternative Medicine (NCCAM). Retrieved on 2007-11-11.
8. Nash, R. A. (2005). Metals in medicine. Alternative Therapies in Health and Medicine , 11 (4), 18-25.
9. Bridges, S. (2006). The promise of chelation. Mothering , 54-61.
10. Ernst E (2000). "Chelation therapy for coronary heart disease: An overview of all clinical investigations". *Am. Heart J.* 140 (1): 139–41. doi:10.1067/mhj.2000.107548. PMID 10874275.
11. Weber W, Newmark S (2007). "Complementary and alternative medical therapies for attention-deficit/hyperactivity disorder and autism". *Pediatr Clin North Am* 54 (6): 983–1006. doi:10.1016/j.pcl.2007.09.006. PMID 18061787.
12. Bernard S, Enayati A, Roger H, Binstock T, Redwood L (2002). "The role of mercury in the pathogenesis of autism" (PDF). *Mol Psychiatry* 7 (Suppl 2): S42–3. doi:10.1038/sj.mp.4001177 (inactive 2008-09-08). PMID 12142947.
13. Altug, T. (2003). Introduction to Toxicology and Food. Boca Raton, FL, CRC *Press.*
14. Body Burden: The Pollution in People. Environmental Working Group, www.ewg.com, 2003.
15. Houlihan J., Kropp T, et al. (2005). Body Burden: The Pollution in Newborns. Washington, DC, Environmental Working Group: 76.
16. Cutler, A.H. (2004). Hair Test Interpretation: Finding Hidden Toxicities. Seattle, WA, Self Published.
17. Dentist the Menace? The Uncontrolled Release of Dental Mercury. Mercury Policy Project, Health Care Without Harm, Sierra Club, et al., June 2002.
18. http://maps.grida.no/go/graphic/mercury_levels_in_indigenous_women.

19. "Arsenic Compounds." Tenth Report on Carcinogen. U.S. Department of Health and Human Services, Public Health Service, National Toxicology Program, December 2002.
20. Screening Young Children for Lead Poisoning: Guidance for State and Local Public Health Officials. U.S. Center for Disease Control and Prevention, 1997.
21. Report on the National Survey of Lead-Based Paint in Housing, Base Report, U.S. Environmental Protection Agency, Office of Pollution, Prevention and Toxics, April 1995.
22. What Every Parent Should Know About Lead Poisoning in Children. U.S. Centers for Disease Prevention and Control.
23. Jacobs, David E. "The Healthy Effects of Lead on the Human Body," Lead Perspectives Magazine (November/December 1996).